JOHN LE NEVE

Fasti Ecclesiae Anglicanae

1300–1541

JOHN LE NEVE

Fasti Ecclesiae Anglicanae
1300-1541

VIII
Bath and Wells Diocese

COMPILED BY B. JONES

UNIVERSITY OF LONDON
INSTITUTE OF HISTORICAL RESEARCH
THE ATHLONE PRESS
1964

Published by
THE ATHLONE PRESS
UNIVERSITY OF LONDON
at 2 Gower Street, London WC1
Distributed by Constable & Co. Ltd
12 *Orange Street, London* WC2

Canada
Oxford University Press
Toronto

U.S.A.
Oxford University Press Inc
New York

Printed in Great Britain by
WESTERN PRINTING SERVICES LTD
BRISTOL

Foreword

WORK on the diocese of Bath and Wells has presented a number of difficulties and in many cases the lists of prebendaries and dignitaries are very fragmentary and sketchy, because of the many gaps in the cathedral records at Wells and in the series of bishops' registers. The registers of bishops Barnet, Harewell, Skirlaw and Erghum have been lost which has meant a scarcity of precise information for the period 1363–1400. This fourteenth-century gap is not as serious as that of the sixteenth century since for the former century cathedral registers and the Calendars of Patent Rolls and Papal Letters have been available as supplementary sources of information. The scarcity of any records in the sixteenth century has proved a serious handicap; John Clerke was bishop of Wells 1523–1541 but his register does not extend beyond 1527, and the register of bishop Barlow, 1548–1553, has been lost. There is an almost complete dearth of cathedral records for the greater part of the sixteenth century, since the chapter acts, calendared by the Historical Manuscripts Commission, extend from 1487 to 1513, and start again in 1571. Owing to this lack of records for the sixteenth century it has been necessary to use the *Valor Ecclesiasticus* extensively, and for some of the prebends this has proved the only source of information until the end of the century. The series of Ledger Books which cover a period 1523–1813, and which are to be found in the chapter library at Wells, have not been of any assistance in making the lists of prebendaries, since the material consists mainly of copies of leases granted by the chapter during this period. No attempt was made in Hardy's edition of Le Neve's *Fasti Ecclesiae Anglicanae* to list the Wells prebendaries, except in the case of prebendaries of St Decumans, before the time of the *Valor*. Some information about the prebendaries of Wells 1300–1541 has been obtained from the registers of other bishops, since three of the prebends of Wells were situated in other dioceses, Holcombe in Exeter, Shalford in London and Warminster al. Luxville in Salisbury, and from examination of the registers of these dioceses further information has been obtained.

B.J.

Contents

References

WORKS IN PRINT

CCR. — *Calendar of the Close Rolls preserved in the Public Record Office.* 55 vols. London, 1892–1955.

CPL. — *Calendar of Entries in the Papal Registers relating to Great Britain and Ireland: Papal letters.* 14 vols. in 15. London, 1893–1960.

CPP. — *Calendar of Entries in the Papal Registers relating to Great Britain and Ireland: Petitions to the Pope, 1342–1419.* Vol. i. London, 1896.

CPR. — *Calendar of the Patent Rolls preserved in the Public Record Office.* London, 1891–1937.

Cal. MSS. D. & C. Wells. — *Calendar of the Manuscripts of the Dean and Chapter of Wells.* 2 vols. Historical Manuscripts Commission, 1907–14.

Chartularies of Bath. — *Two chartularies of the priory of St Peter at Bath: i, the chartulary in MS. No. CXI in the library of Corpus Christi College, Cambridge; ii, calendar of the MS. register in the library of the Hon. Society of Lincoln's Inn,* ed. W. Hunt. Somerset Record Society, vii, 1893.

Emden, Reg. Ox. — *Biographical Register of the University of Oxford to 1500,* comp. A. B. Emden. 3 vols. Oxford, 1957–9.

Eubel. — *Hierarchia Catholica Medii Aevi,* ed. C. Eubel. 3 vols. Münster, 1913–23.

L. & P. — *Letters and Papers of the Reign of Henry VIII,* ed. J. S. Brewer. London, 1862–1932.

R.S.A. — *Registrum Sacrum Anglicanum,* by W. Stubbs. Oxford, 1897.

Reg. Bekynton. — *The Register of Thomas Bekynton, bishop of Bath and Wells, 1443–1465,* ed. H. C. Maxwell-Lyte and M. C. B. Dawes. 2 vols. Somerset Record Society, xlix, l, 1934–5.

Reg. Bps., 1518–1559. — *The Registers of Thomas Wolsey, bishop of Bath and Wells, 1518–1523; John Clerke, bishop of Bath and Wells, 1523–1541; William Knyght, bishop of Bath and Wells, 1541–1547; and Gilbert Bourne, bishop of Bath and Wells, 1554–1559,* ed. Sir Henry Maxwell-Lyte. Somerset Record Society, lv, 1940.

Reg. Bubwith. — *The Register of Nicholas Bubwith, bishop of Bath and Wells, 1407–1424,* ed. T. S. Holmes. 2 vols. Somerset Record Society, xxix, xxx, 1913–14.

Reg. Drokensford. — *Calendar of the Register of John de Drokensford, bishop of Bath and Wells, 1309–1329,* ed. E. Hobhouse. Somerset Record Society, 1887.

Reg. Gandavo. *Registrum Simonis de Gandavo, diocesis Saresbiriensis, 1297–1315*, ed. C. T. Flower and M. C. B. Dawes. 1 vol. in 2. Canterbury and York Society, xl, xli, 1934.

Reg. Giffard and Bowet. *The Registers of Walter Giffard, bishop of Bath and Wells, 1265–6 and of Henry Bowett, bishop of Bath and Wells, 1401–1407,* ed. T. S. Holmes. Somerset Record Society, xiii, 1899.

Reg. Gilbert. *Registrum Johannis Gilbert, episcopi Herefordensis, 1375–1389,* ed. J. H. Parry. Canterbury and York Society, xviii, 1915.

Reg. King. *The Registers of Oliver King, bishop of Bath and Wells, 1496–1503 and Hadrian de Castello, bishop of Bath and Wells, 1503–1518,* ed. H. C. Maxwell-Lyte. Somerset Record Society, liv, 1939.

Reg. Langham. *Registrum Simonis Langham, Cantuariensis archiepiscopi,* ed. A. C. Wood. Canterbury and York Society, liii, 1956.

Reg. R. de Salopia. *The Register of Ralph of Shrewsbury, bishop of Bath and Wells, 1329–1363,* ed. T. S. Holmes. 2 vols. Somerset Record Society, ix, x, 1896.

Reg. Stafford (Bath and Wells). *The Register of John Stafford, bishop of Bath and Wells, 1425–1443,* ed. T. S. Holmes. Somerset Record Society, xxxi, xxxii, 1915–16.

Reg. Stillington. *The Registers of Robert Stillington, bishop of Bath and Wells, 1466–1491 and Richard Fox, bishop of Bath and Wells, 1492–1494,* ed. H. C. Maxwell-Lyte. Somerset Record Society, lii, 1937.

Reg. Sudbury. *Registrum Simonis de Sudbiria, diocesis Londoniensis, 1362–1375,* ed. R. C. Fowler. 2 vols. Canterbury and York Society, xxxiv, xxxviii, 1927–38.

Reg. Winchelsey. *Registrum Roberti Winchelsey, Cantuariensis archiepiscopi, 1294–1313,* ed. R. Graham. 1 vol. in 2. Canterbury and York Society, li, lii, 1952–6.

Som. Med. Wills. *Somerset Medieval Wills,* ed. F. W. Weaver. [First series,] 1383–1500. Second series, 1501–1530. Third series, 1531-1558. Somerset Record Society, xvi, xix, xxi, 1901–5.

VCH. *The Victoria History of the Counties of England.*

Valor. *Valor Ecclesiasticus temp. Henr. VIII.* 6 vols. 1810–25.

Wharton. *Anglia Sacra,* comp. H. Wharton. 2 vols. London, 1691.

IN MANUSCRIPT

Wells Diocesan Registry
Registers of bishops Drokensford, 1309–29, and King, 1496–1503.

Wells Cathedral Library
MSS. of the Dean and Chapter.
   Register I.
   Liber Ruber.

Lambeth Palace Library
Registers of the archbishops of Canterbury.

Somerset House
PCC: Registers of wills proved in the prerogative court of Canterbury.

Note
  Dr A. B. Emden's *Biographical Register of the University of Oxford to 1500* has been followed for degrees. But some later medieval bishops' registers and chapter act books give the title of *magister* to B.A.s. This anomalous title appears in this edition of the *Fasti*, when there is manuscript authority for it.

Abbreviations

The following abbreviations are given in lower case or in capitals as required

abp. archbishop
adm. admission, admit, admitted
archdcn. archdeacon
archdcnry archdeaconry
B.C.L. bachelor of civil law
B.Cn.L. bachelor of canon law
B.M. bachelor of medicine
B.Mus. bachelor of music
B.Th. bachelor of theology
bp. bishop
bpc. bishopric
c. *circa*
can. canon
card. cardinal
cath. cathedral
certif. certificate
ch. church
chap. chapel
chapt. chapter
coll. collation, collated
colleg. collegiate
comm. commission
conf. confirmation, confirmed
cons. consecration, consecrated
ct. court
d. death, died
d. and c. dean and chapter
D.C.L. doctor of civil law
dcn. deacon
depriv. deprived
dioc. diocese
dn. dean
ed. edition, edited by
el. election, elect, elected
exch. exchange, exchanged
excomm. excommunication, excommuni-
   cated
f. folio

gr. grant, granted
instal. installation, installed
judgt. judgment
k. king
Lamb. Lambeth
lic. licence
lic. *alibi cons.* licence *alibi consecrari*
Lic.C.L. licentiate in civil law
lic. el. licence to elect
M. *magister*, master
M.A. master of arts
mand. mandate
mand. adm. mandate to admit
n.d. no date
O.Can.S.A. order of Augustinian canons
O.Cist. order of Cistercians
O.F.M. order of Friars Minor
O.S.B. order of St Benedict
O.St.J. of Jer. order of St. John of
   Jerusalem
occ. occurrence, occurs
P.R.O. Public Record Office
pr. priest
preb. prebend, prebendary
pres. presentation, present, presented
prohibn. prohibition
prov. provision, provided
ratif. ratification, ratified
reg. register
res. resignation, resigned
reservn. reservation
s.d. same day
Salis. Salisbury
Sch.C.L. scholar of civil law
spir. spiritualities
temps. temporalities
trans. translation, translated
vac. vacancy, vacant, vacated

Bath and Wells 1300–1541

BISHOPS

William de Marcia 1292–1302.

Lic. el. sought 25 Nov. 1292 at Wells, 27 Nov. at Bath (P.R.O., C 84/11/3 & 5). Gr. 16 Dec. (*CPR. 1292–1301* p. 2). El. 28 Jan. 1293 (*Cal. MSS. D. & C. Wells* I 529). Petition for royal assent 31 Jan. (P.R.O., C 84/11/10). Royal assent 1 March (*CPR. 1292–1301* p. 6). Profession to Canterbury 12 March (Cant., Reg. A f. 205b/218b). Temps. 19 March (*CPR. 1292–1301* p. 8). Cons. 17 May (Cant., Reg. A f. 205b/218b). D. before 19 June 1302 (*Reg. Winchelsey* I 438).

Walter de Haselschawe 1302–1308.

Lic. el. gr. 29 June 1302 (*CPR. 1301–1307* p. 41). Mand. by abp. 5 July to el. suitable person (*Reg. Winchelsey* I 440). El. 7 Aug. (P.R.O., C 84/14/30). Petition by chapt. at Wells for royal assent 9 Aug., by prior and chapt. of Bath 10 Aug. (P.R.O., C 84/14/30 & 31). Royal assent 13 Aug. (*CPR. 1301–1307* p. 53). Assent of abp. 11 Sept. (*Reg. Winchelsey* II 769). Temps. 12 Sept. (*CPR. 1301–1307* p. 62). Cons. 4 Nov. (*Reg. Winchelsey* II 770–1). D. 11 Dec. 1308 (*ibid.* p. 1077).

John de Drokensford 1309–1329.

Lic. el. sought 19 Dec. 1308 by the chapt. at Bath (P.R.O., C 84/16/14). Gr. 25 Dec. (*CPR. 1307–1313* p. 97). El. 5 Feb. 1309 (P.R.O., C 84/16/15). Petition for royal assent 7 Feb. (*ibid.*). Royal assent 23 Feb. (*CPR. 1307–1313* p. 100). Temps. 15 May (*ibid.* p. 114). Cons. 9 Nov. at Canterbury (Cant., Reg. A f. 205b/218b).[1] Mand. to enthrone 30 Nov. 1310 (*Reg. Drokensford* p. 37). D. 9 May 1329 (*Reg. R. de Salopia* I p. xvii).

M. **Ralph de Salopia** D.Th., D.Cn.L. 1329–1363.

Lic. el. gr. 23 May 1329 (*CPR. 1327–1330* p. 391). Royal assent 28 June (*ibid.* p. 402). Temps. 22 July (*ibid.* p. 409). Cons. 3 Sept. (*R.S.A.*). D. 14 Aug. 1363 (*Reg. R. de Salopia* I p. xxxvi).

[M. **Philip de Beauchamp** 1363.]
[**Walter de Monyngton** O.S.B. 1363.]
M. **John Barnet** B.C.L. 1363–1366.

Lic. el. gr. 4 Sept. 1363 (*CPR. 1361–1364* p. 387). Beauchamp's el. set aside 28 Nov. because under age (*CPL.* IV 5). Monyngton el. some time after d. of Salopia (*Wharton* I 569). 9 Jan. 1364, mand. by abp. to guardian of bpc. of Wells to revoke sentence against prior and chapt. of Bath for disobedience to his monition to forward to chapt. of Wells the decree of el. of Monyngton as bp. (*Cal. MSS. D. & C. Wells* I 266). Barnet trans. from Worcester 24 Dec. 1363 (Lamb., Reg. Islip f. 244b). Temps. 6 Apr. 1364 (*CPR. 1361–1364* p. 477). Spir. 7 Apr. (Lamb., Reg. Islip f. 244b). Bp. of Ely 1366.

---

[1] The date of the cons. of bp. Drokensford is given as 10 Aug. 1309 (*Reg. Henrici Woodlock*, ed. A. W. Goodman (Canterbury and York Soc., xliii, xliv) I 382), but the date given in the Canterbury register, 9 Nov., is probably correct since bp. Drokensford was cons. at Canterbury.

M. **John de Harewell** B.C.L. 1366–1386.

Prov. 14 Dec. 1366 (*Eubel* I 133). Lic. *alibi cons.* 14 Jan. 1367 (*CPL.* IV 60). Cons. 7 March (*R.S.A.*). Gr. issues of temps. from 29 Apr. 1367, 20 Feb. 1368 (*CPR. 1367–1370* p. 90). Temps. 6 March 1369 (*ibid.* p. 225). Profession to Canterbury 25 Oct. 1371 (Lamb., Reg. Wittlesey f. 127). D. 29 June/14 July 1386 (*Som. Med. Wills 1501–1530* p. 90; P.R.O., C 84/33/49).

[Richard de Medeford 1386.]

M. **Walter de Skirlaw** D.Cn.L. 1386–1388.

Lic. el. sought by prior of Bath 14 July 1386, by dn. of Wells 15 July (P.R.O., C 84/33/49 & 50). Gr. 16 July (*CPR. 1385–1389* p. 199). Petition for royal assent to el. of Medeford 10 Aug. (P.R.O., C 84/35/43). Royal assent signified to pope 15 Aug. (*CPR. 1385–1389* p. 207). El. set aside by trans. of Skirlaw from Coventry and Lichfield 18 Aug. (Lamb., Reg. Courtenay f. 321b). Temps. 13 Sept. and 3 Nov. (*CPR. 1385–1389* p. 241). Bp. of Durham 1388.

M. **Ralph Erghum** D.Cn. & C.L. 1388–1400.

Trans. from Salisbury 3 Apr. 1388 (*Cal. MSS. D. & C. Wells* I 299). Temps. 13 Sept. (*CPR. 1385–1389* p. 504). Profession to Canterbury 14 Sept. (Lamb., Reg. Courtenay f. 322). Spir. 15 Sept. (*ibid.*). D. 10 Apr. 1400 (*Emden, Reg. Ox.* I 645).

M. **Richard Clifford** *senior* 1400–1401.

Lic. el. sought 22 Apr. 1400 at Wells, 23 Apr. at Bath (P.R.O., C 84/38/13 & 14). Clifford prov. 12 May (*CPL.* V 287). Lic. *alibi cons.* 13 May (*ibid.* p. 269). Bp. of Worcester 1401.

M. **Henry Bowet** D.Cn. & C.L. 1401–1407.

Prov. 19 Aug. 1401 (Lamb., Reg. Arundell I f. 11b). Temps. 21 Sept. (*CPR. 1399–1401* p. 547). Profession to Canterbury 28 Sept. (Lamb., Reg. Arundell I f. 12). Lic. *alibi cons.* 12 Nov. (Cant., Reg. T f. 46). Cons. 15 Nov. (*Reg. Giffard and Bowet* p. 14). Abp. of York 1407.

Nicholas Bubwith 1407–1424.

Trans. from Salisbury 7 Oct. 1407 (Lamb., Reg. Arundell I f. 40). Temps. 2 Dec. (*CPR. 1405–1408* p. 383). Spir. 1 Apr. 1408 (*Reg. Bubwith* I 23). D. 27 Oct. 1424 (*ibid.* p. xxx).

M. **John Stafford** D.C.L. 1424–1443.

Lic. el. gr. 14 Nov. 1424 (*CPR. 1422–1429* p. 254). El. notified to k. by chapt. at Wells 19 Dec., by chapt. at Bath 20 Dec. (P.R.O., C 84/43/9 & 10). Prov. 18 Dec. (*CPL.* VII 408). Royal assent 26 Dec. (*CPR. 1422–1429* p. 265). Temps. 12 May 1425 (*ibid.* p. 274). Cons. 27 May (*R.S.A.*). Profession to Canterbury 31 May (*Reg. of H. Chichele*, ed. E. F. Jacob (Canterbury and York Soc., xlii, xlv–xlvii) I 87–8). Abp. of Canterbury 1443.

M. **Thomas Bekynton** D.C.L. 1443–1465.

Prov. 24 July 1443 (*CPL.* IX 342). Lic. *alibi cons.* 30 July (*ibid.* p. 336). Lic. *alibi cons.* requested from abp. by k. 2 Sept., gr. 7 Sept. (Cant., Reg. S ff. 154b–155). Temps. 24 Sept. (*CPR. 1441–1446* p. 205). Cons. 13 Oct. (*Reg. Bekynton* I 1). Spir. 15 Oct. (Lamb., Reg. Stafford f. 9). D. 14 Jan. 1465 (*Emden, Reg. Ox.* I 158).

[M. **John Phreas** *or* **Free** D.M. 1465.]

M. **Robert Stillington** D.C.L. 1465–1491.

Custody of temps. gr. to Stillington 20 Jan. 1465 (*CPR. 1461–1467* p. 387). Lic. el. gr. 19 Feb. (*ibid.* p. 386). Phreas el. 1465 but d. in Sept. before cons. (*Wharton* I 574;

Emden, Reg. Ox. II 725). Stillington prov. 30 Oct. (*CPL.* XII 519). Lic. *alibi cons.* 31 Oct. (*ibid.*). Spir. 11 Jan. 1466 (*Reg. Stillington* p. 1). Temps. 29 Jan. (*CPR. 1461–1467* p. 477). Cons. 16 March (*Reg. Stillington* p. 2). D. May 1491 (*ibid.* p. xiv).

M. **Richard Fox** D.C.L. 1492–1494.

Trans. from Exeter 8 Feb. 1492 (Lamb., Reg. Morton I ff. 23b–24). Temps. 4 May (*CPR. 1485–1494* p. 379). Bp. of Durham 1494.

M. **Oliver King** D.Cn. & C.L. 1495–1503.

Trans. from Exeter 6 Nov. 1495 (*Cal. MSS. D. & C. Wells* II 143). Temps. 6 Jan. 1496 (*CPR. 1494–1509* p. 47). Enthroned after 12 March (*Cal. MSS. D. & C. Wells* II 144). D. 29 Aug. 1503 (*ibid.* p. 171).

Hadrian de Castello Card. pr. of S. Chrysogonus. 1504–1518.

Trans. from Hereford 2 Aug. 1504 (Lamb., Reg. Warham I f. 9). Temps. 13 Oct. (*CPR. 1494–1509* p. 400). Enthroned by proxy 20 Oct. (*Cal. MSS. D. & C. Wells* II 180). Profession to Canterbury n.d. (Lamb., Reg. Warham I f. 8b). Depriv. 5 July 1518 (*L. & P.* II ii No. 4289).

M. **Thomas Wolsey** D.Th. Card. pr. of S. Caecilia. 1518–1523.

Prov. to hold bpc. *in commendam* with Lincoln 27 July 1518 (P.R.O., Papal Bulls 26 (34)). Custody of temps. gr. 26 and 28 Aug. (*L. & P.* II ii No. 4397). Bp. of Durham 1523.

M. **John Clerke** D.C.L. 1523–1541.

Prov. 26 March 1523 (*L. & P.* III ii No. 3003). Temps. 2 May (*ibid.*). Cons. 6 Dec. (*R.S.A.*). D. 31 Jan. 1541 (Lamb., Reg. Cranmer f. 266).

M. **William Knight** D.C.L. 1541–1547.

Lic. el. sought 8 Feb. 1541 (*Cal. MSS. D. & C. Wells* II 253). Gr. 9 Apr. (*ibid.*). El. of Knight notified to k. 23 Apr. (*ibid.*). Royal assent 5 May (*L. & P.* XVI No. 878 (29)). Assent of abp. 19 May (Lamb., Reg. Cranmer f. 261). Cons. 29 May (*ibid.* f. 269b). Temps. 30 May (*L. & P.* XVI No. 878 (82)). D. 29 Sept. 1547 (*Emden, Reg. Ox.* II 1064).

DEANS

Note: The prebend of Wedmore Prima was attached to the deanery.

Walter de Haselschawe ?–1302.

Occ. 8 Aug. 1299 (*CPR. 1292–1301* p. 472). Bp. of Bath and Wells 1302.

M. **Henry Husee** 1302–?

El. 1302 (*Wharton* I 589).

John de Godeley ?–1333.

Occ. 18 Dec. 1305 (*CPL.* II 7). D. before 9 Feb. 1333 (*Reg. R. de Salopia* I 137).

Richard de Bury *or* d'Aungerville *or* de Sancto Edmundo 1333.

Lic. el. sought 9 Feb. 1333 (*Reg. R. de Salopia* I 137). Gr. 11 Feb. (*ibid.*). Adm. by bp. 20 Feb. (*ibid.*). Bp. of Durham in Oct.

M. **Wibert de Lutleton** B.C.L. 1334–1335.
M. **Robert de Stratford** M.A. 1334–1336.
Walter de London 1335–1349.
Robert Mortimer 1337.

El. of Lutleton as dn. notified to bp. 22 Apr. 1334 (*Reg. R. de Salopia* I 166). Bp. cited opposers of el. to appear 11 June (*ibid.* pp. 166–7). Prov. of Stratford to deanery

6 Aug. (*CPL.* II 402). Petition by chapt. at Wells to curia on behalf of Lutleton 16 Jan. 1335 (*Cal. MSS. D. & C. Wells* I 235). Royal gr. of deanery to London before 20 Jan. (*Reg. R. de Salopia* I 183–4). Lutleton d. before 20 Aug. (*Cal. MSS. D. & C. Wells* I 236) and Stratford obtained archdcnry of Canterbury 1336 and res. claim to deanery. Profession to bp. by London 14 Oct. 1336 (*Reg. R. de Salopia* I 277). Mortimer occ. as dn. 4 June 1337 (*CCR. 1337–1339* p. 135). Probably a scribal error since he was then archdcn. of Wells. London occ. as dn. at d., before 25 Jan. 1349 (*CPP.* I 145).

M. **Thomas Fastolf** D.C.L. 1349–1350.
Prov. 25 Jan. 1349 (*CPP.* I 145). Res. before 28 May 1350 (*ibid.* p. 197).

M. **John de Carleton** D.C.L. 1350–1361.
Prov. 28 May 1350 (*CPP.* I 197). D. before 27 Aug. 1361 (*Cal. MSS. D. & C. Wells* I 263).

William de Cammel 1361.
M. **William de Loughteburgh** D.C.L. 1361.
M. **Stephen de Pempel** D.C.L. 1361–1379.
M. **Thomas de Paxton** D.C.L. 1362.
Lic. el. gr. 27 Aug. 1361 (*Cal. MSS. D. & C. Wells* I 263). K. recommended Loughteburgh as dn. 6 Sept. (*ibid.* p. 264). Chapt. replied, 28 Sept. that Cammel had already been el. (*ibid.*). Cammel refused appointment (*ibid.*) Chapt. convened for el. 13 Oct. (*ibid.*). El. of Pempel 3 Nov. (*ibid.*). Request for conf. by bp. 4 Nov. (*ibid.* p. 265). Paxton prov. before d. of pope Innocent VI, i.e. before 12 Sept. 1362 (*CPP.* I 395). Petitioned pope Urban V for conf. of prov. 11 Nov. (*ibid.*). Did not obtain possession of deanery, Pempel d. as dn. 2 Feb. 1379 (*Cal. MSS. D. & C. Wells* I 281).

John de Fordham 1379–1381.
Lic. el. gr. 11 Feb. 1379 (*Cal. MSS. D. & C. Wells* I 282). El. 22 Feb. (*ibid.* p. 283). Request for bp's conf. of el. 4 March (*ibid.* p. 284). Mand. to install 9 March (*ibid.* p. 287). Bp. of Durham 1381.

M. **Thomas Thebaud de Sudbury** D.C.L. ?–1396.
Occ. 2 Jan. 1384 (*Cal. MSS. D. & C. Wells* I 293). D. before 16 Oct. 1396 (*CPR. 1396–1399* p. 34).[1]

M. **Henry Beaufort** M.A. 1396–1398.
Royal permission to execute prov. to deanery, 20 Dec. 1396 (*CPR. 1396–1399* p. 46). Royal gr. 5 Jan. 1397 (*ibid.* p. 49). Bp. of Lincoln 1398.

Henry de Minutulis Card. pr. of S. Anastasia. 1398–?
Prov. 27 Feb. 1398 (*CPL.* V 112).

Nicholas Slake ?–1401.
Thomas Tuttebury 1401–1410.
Thomas de Stanley 1402, 1403.
Slake occ. as dn. 9 Oct. 1398 (*CPR. 1396–1399* p. 426). Prov. 25 Jan. 1400 (*CPL.* V 284). Tuttebury coll. by abp. 24 Feb. 1401 (Lamb., Reg. Arundell I f. 279). Comm. appointed by abp. to enquire into claims of Slake to deanery (*ibid.*). Mand. to install Tuttebury 26 Nov. (*Reg. Giffard and Bowet* p. 21). Royal gr. to Tuttebury 19 June 1402 (*CPR. 1401–1405* p. 101). Royal prohibn. 14 Sept. to chapt. at Wells against persons acting contrary to royal statutes, 25 Edward III and 13 Richard II (*ibid.*

---

[1] The k. tried to secure the el. of Guy de Mona as dn. (*Anglo-Norman Letters and Petitions* ed. M. D. Legge (Oxford, 1941) pp. 238–9). Le Neve-Hardy states that he was el. on 10 Aug. 1396 but no evidence has been found for this.

p. 136). Stanley then claiming deanery by prov. against claims of Tuttebury, k's clerk (*ibid.*). Stanley had been lately prov. 23 Apr. 1403 (*CPL.* V 534). Did not obtain possession as Tuttebury d. as dn. before 3 Apr. 1410 (*Reg. Bubwith* I 78).

M. **Richard Courtenay** B.C.L. 1410–1413.
Lic. el. sought 3 Apr. 1410 (*Reg. Bubwith* I 78). Gr. 10 Apr. (*ibid.* II 466–7). El. 26 May (*ibid.* p. 472). Mand. adm. 19 June (*ibid.* pp. 474–7). Bp. of Norwich 1413.

Thomas Karneka 1413.
Deanery reserved for Karneka 28 June 1413 (*CPL.* VI 433). D. as dn. before 25 Sept. (*Reg. Bubwith* I 147).

M. **Walter de Medeford** B.Cn. & C.L. 1413–1423.
Lic. el. sought 25 Sept. 1413 (*Reg. Bubwith* I 147). El. conf. 8 Nov. (*ibid.* II 480). D. before 14 July 1423 (*Som. Med. Wills 1501–1530* pp. 320–5).

M. **John Stafford** D.C.L. 1423–1424.
Lic. el. gr. 28 July 1423 (*Reg. Bubwith* II 484). El. conf. 9 Sept. (*ibid.* p. 483). Bp. of Bath and Wells 1424.

John Forest 1425–1446.
Lic. el. sought 20 July 1425 (*Reg. Stafford (Bath and Wells)* II 284–5). Gr. 1 Aug. (*ibid.* p. 285). Comm. by bp. 18 Nov. to confirm el. (*ibid.* p. 286). Mand. to install 19 Nov. (*ibid.*). D. 25 March 1446 (*Reg. Bekynton* II 430).[1]

M. **John Delaberd** B.Cn.L. 1446.
M. **Nicholas Carent** Lic.C.L. 1446–1467.
Lic. el. sought 28 March 1446 (*Reg. Bekynton* II 432). Gr. 1 Apr. (*ibid.*). Delaberd received royal gr. of pardon, 30 May, for accepting prov. to deanery (*CPR. 1441–1446* p. 447). Gr. lic. to sue for title 16 July (*ibid.* p. 442). Carent el. dn. by chapt. 22 Aug. (*Reg. Bekynton* II 430). Conf. by bp. (*ibid.* pp. 430–3). Complaint by Delaberd 3 Oct. that unable to obtain possession of deanery (*CPL.* VIII 273–4). Bp. protested, 17 March 1447, that Delaberd had never exhibited prov. to deanery (*Reg. Beyknton* II 434). Prov. to bpc. of St Davids in Sept. Carent d. before 2 Nov. 1467 (PCC 20 Godyn), but must have res. earlier in the year.[2]

M. **William Witham** D.C.L. 1467–1472.
Occ. 26 July 1467 (*Cal. MSS. D. & C. Wells* II 685). D. before 28 Sept. 1472 (*Reg. Stillington* p. 94).

M. **John Gunthorpe** 1472–1498.
Lic. el. sought 28 Sept. 1472 (*Reg. Stillington* p. 94). Gr. 5 Oct. (*ibid.*). Assent of bp. to el. 19 Jan. 1473 (*ibid.* p. 96). D. 25 June 1498 (*Reg. King* p. 85).

M. **William Cosyn** Lic.C.L. 1498–1525.
El. 20 Dec. 1498 (*Reg. King* p. 85). Conf. by bp. 15 Apr. 1499 (*ibid.* p. 86). Instal. in person 8 June 1502 (*Cal. MSS. D. & C. Wells* II 167). Res. c. Dec. 1525 (*L. & P.* IV i No. 1790).[3]

[1] 6 July is given in the Canterbury obit (Lambeth Palace MS. 20 f. 198b) as the date of d. of John Forest, dn. of Wells, but the Wells register seems the more accurate source.
[2] There is no evidence that Henry Webber was dn. for a short time after the d. of Carent (*Wharton* I 590). There has possibly been confusion because a Henry Webber was then dn. of Exeter, 1459–1477.
[3] Polydore Vergil occ. as dn. of Wells 1 June 1515 (*L. & P.* II i No. 546). This is probably a scribal error since he was then archdcn. of Wells.

M. Thomas Winter 1525–1529.

El. of Winter requested by card. Wolsey, 28 Nov. 1525 (*L. & P.* IV i No. 1790). Chapt. replied that deanery would be vac. by Christmas (*ibid.*). Occ. as dn. 12 Apr. 1529 and 30 June (*ibid.* ii No. 2054).

M. Richard Woleman D.Cn.L. 1529–1537.

Occ. 1529 (*L. & P.* IV iii No. 6047 p. 2697). D. before 19 Sept. 1537 (*ibid.* XII ii No. 720).

Thomas Cromwell 1537–1540.

Lic. el. sought 23 Sept. 1537 (*Cal. MSS. D. & C. Wells* II 247). El. of Cromwell conf. by bp. 26 Sept. (*L. & P.* XII ii No. 753). Executed 28/29 July 1540 (T. Holingshed, *Chronicles* (1807) III 817; *L. & P.* XV No. 926).

William Fitzjames *or* Fitzwilliams 1540–1548.

Lic. el. sought 2 Nov. 1540 (*Cal. MSS. D. & C. Wells* II 252). Gr. 3 Dec. (*ibid.* pp. 252–3). Res. before 7 Jan. 1548, then called Thomas (*CPR. 1547–1548* p. 192).

PRECENTORS

Thomas de Gorges ?–1316.

Occ. 8 Apr. 1297 (*CPR. 1292–1301* p. 276). D. before 8 March 1316 (*Reg. Drokensford* p. 124).

M. Thomas de Dylyngton D.Th. 1316–?

Coll. 8 March 1316 (*Reg. Drokensford* p. 124).

Richard de Thistleden ?–1327.

Occ. 1 Jan. 1326 (*Reg. Drokensford* p. 238). Treasurer 1327.

Richard de Drokensford 1327.

Coll. 10 June 1327 (*Reg. Drokensford* p. 271). Exch. precentorship with William de Bokland for ch. of Ewell, Surr., 12 Aug. (Winchester, Reg. Stratford f. 103).

William de Bokland 1327–?

By exch. Aug. 1327. Mand. adm. 18 Aug. (Winchester, Reg. Stratford f. 103). Occ. 25 Sept. 1333 (Reg. I f. 193).

Richard de Carleton ?–1335.

Exch. precentorship with William de Littleton for ch. of Uffculme, Devon, 20 Dec. 1335 (*Reg. R. de Salopia* I 251–2).

M. William de Littleton 1335–1355.

By exch. Dec. 1335. D. before 30 Jan. 1355 (*CPP.* I 276).

M. Edmund Gournay Sch.C.L. 1355–?

Prov. 30 Jan. 1355 (*CPP.* I 276). Probably held precentorship until 1361 when preb. of Wormenstre.

William de Cammel ?–1386.

Occ. 18 Dec. 1361 (*CPR. 1361–1364* p. 348). D. 20 March 1386 (P.R.O., C 84/33/37).

M. John Trevaur B.C.L. 1386–1392.

Estate ratif. 14 Aug. 1386 (*CPR. 1385–1389* p. 208). Exch. precentorship and preb. of Combe Undecima with John Mere for ch. of Meifod, Montgom., 18 July 1392 (*CPR. 1391–1396* p. 122).

John Mere 1392–?
By exch. July 1392.

M. **Ralph Erghum** ?–1410.
Estate ratif. 4 Oct. 1397 (*CPR. 1396–1399* p. 199) and 1 Sept. 1401 (*CPR. 1399–1401* p. 483). D. 3/8 March 1410 (PCC 21 Marche; *Reg. Bubwith* I 5).

M. **John Hody** B.C.L. 1410–1426.
Coll. 12 May 1410 (*Reg. Bubwith* I 5, 9). Chancellor 1426.

M. **John Storthwayt** B.C.L. 1427–1440.
Coll. 10 Feb. 1427 (*Reg. Stafford (Bath and Wells)* I 44). Chancellor 1440.

William Stephens 1440–1447.
Coll. 28 March 1440 (*Reg. Stafford (Bath and Wells)* II 247). D. 27/30 June 1447 (*Som. Med. Wills 1383–1500* pp. 157–9; *Reg. Bekynton* I 79).

M. **John Bernard** B.Cn.L. 1447–1451.
Coll. 8 Nov. 1447 (*Reg. Bekynton* I 83–4). Treasurer 1451.

M. **Thomas Boleyn** 1451–1472.
Coll. 25 Oct. 1451 (*Reg. Bekynton* I 171). D. before 19 Feb. 1472 (*Reg. Stillington* p. 91).

M. **Thomas Overary** B.C.L. 1472–1493.
Adm. 19 Feb. 1472 (*Reg. Stillington* p. 91). D. 18/28 July 1493 (PCC 4 Vox; *CPR. 1485–1494* p. 430).

M. **William Warham** D.C.L. 1493–1501.
Coll. 2 Nov. 1493 (*Reg. Stillington* p. 187). Adm. 18 Nov. (*Cal. MSS. D. & C. Wells* II 135). Bp. of London 1501.

M. **Thomas Cornish** O. St. J. of Jer., M.A. Bp. of Tine.[1] 1502–1513.
Adm. 4 Sept. 1502 (*Cal. MSS. D. & C. Wells* II 167). D. 31 March/20 July 1513 (PCC 18 Fetiplace).

M. **William Piers** D.C.L. 1513–?
Adm. 17 July 1513 (*Cal. MSS. D. & C. Wells* II 233). Occ. 1535, called Walter (*Valor* I 132).

M. **George Dogyon** M.A. ?–1552/3.
Occ. May 1541 (Lamb., Reg. Cranmer f. 262). D. 1 Oct. 1552/19 Feb. 1553 (*Som. Med. Wills 1531–1558* pp. 141–2).

CHANCELLORS

M. **Henry Husee** 1291.
Occ. 18 March 1291 (*CPL.* I 530). He had lately accepted chancellorship at this date (*ibid.*). Occ. 22 Apr. (*Cal. MSS. D. & C. Wells* I 111). ? Until 1302 when el. dn.

Robert de Haselscawe 1306.
Occ. 17 Jan. 1306 (*CPL.* II 18).

M. **Thomas de Loggoure** D.C.L. 1306–1313.
Occ. 12 May 1306 (*CPR. 1301–1307* p. 440). D. before 24 Nov. 1313 (*Reg. Drokensford* p. 158).

[1] Suffragan of the abp. of Tarsus.

Richard de Drokensford 1313–1316.
Coll. 24 Nov. 1313 (*Reg. Drokensford* p. 158). D. before 9 Sept. 1316 (*ibid.* p. 109).

Thomas de Retford 1316–?
Coll. 9 Sept. 1316 (*Reg. Drokensford* p. 109). Occ. Jan. 1336 (*Reg. R. de Salopia* i 255).

M. John de Middleton 1337.
Coll. 20 Nov. 1337 (*Reg. R. de Salopia* i 314). Exch. chancellorship with Simon de Bristol for ch. of Bleadon, Som., 9 Dec. (*ibid.*).

Simon de Bristol 1337–?
By exch. Dec. 1337. Adm. 15 Dec. (*Reg. R. de Salopia* i 315).

M. William de Littleton 1342.
Occ. 4 May 1342 (*CPR. 1340–1343* p. 424).[1]

M. Thomas Luggore ?–1346.
D. as chancellor before 14 Oct. 1346 (*CPL.* iii 236).

Edmund Bouler 1346–?
M. Richard de Tormeton B.Cn. & C.L. 1346–?
M. John de Carleton D.C.L. 1347–1350.
Bouler prov. 14 Oct. 1346 (*CPL.* iii 236). Tormeton prov. before 7 Dec. (*CPP.* i 123). Royal gr. to Carleton 16 June 1347 (*CPR. 1345–1348* p. 336). Tormeton became treasurer 1348, Bouler gr. k's protection for one year, 11 March while appeals being prosecuted in k's cts. (*CPR. 1348–1350* p. 35). Does not appear to have gained possession, d. before 24 Oct. 1349 (*CPL.* iii 296). Carleton prov. to deanery 1350.

John de Horsington 1366, 1377.
Occ. 18 Nov. 1366 (*Reg. Langham* p. 66) and 1377 (P.R.O., E 179/4/1)—chancellorship had been reserved for him 1 June 1350 (*CPL.* iii 360). ? Held chancellorship until d., Sept. 1381/2 (*Cal. MSS. D. & C. Wells* ii 17).

M. Thomas Spert D.C.L. 1382–1397/8.
Thomas Marton 1386.
Spert adm. 7 Aug. 1382 (*Cal. MSS. D. & C. Wells* i 292). Estate ratif. 2 July 1386 (*CPR. 1385–1389* p. 192). Royal gr. 18 July to Spert (*ibid.* p. 202). Royal gr. to Marton 25 Aug. (*ibid.* p. 206). Marton exch. chancellorship with Spert for ch. of Uffculme, Devon, 15 Oct. (*ibid.* p. 221). Royal comm. 10 Nov. to arrest all persons impugning k's title to pres. Spert to chancellorship after exch. of benefices with Marton (*ibid.* p. 263). Second comm. 14 May 1387 (*ibid.* p. 393). Spert occ. as chancellor 24 May 1391 (*CCR. 1389–1392* pp. 343–4). Probably held office until d. Sept. 1397/6 Jan. 1398 (*Cal. MSS. D. & C. Wells* ii 33; Salis., Reg. Medford f. 59).

Thomas Terry ?–1398.
Exch. chancellorship with Nicholas Daniel for ch. of Symondsbury, Dors., 2 Dec. 1398 (Salis., Reg. Medford f. 62b).

Nicholas Daniel 1398–1406.
By exch. Dec. 1398. Estate ratif. 7 Nov. 1399 (*CPR. 1399–1401* p. 27). Exch. chancellorship with Richard Bruton for ch. of Olveston, Glos., 21 Oct. 1406 (*Reg. Giffard and Bowet* p. 65).

---

[1] Probably a scribal error since Littleton was then precentor.

M. **Richard Bruton** 1406–1417.
By exch. Oct. 1406. Estate ratif. 9 Dec. (*CPR. 1405–1408* p. 244). D. 30 Oct./20 Nov. 1417 (PCC 39 Marche; *Reg. Bubwith* I 293).

M. **Thomas Bubwith** B.Cn. & C.L. 1417–1419.
Coll. 20 Nov. 1417 (*Reg. Bubwith* I 293). Archdcn. of Wells 1419.

Thomas Shelford 1419–1426.
Coll. 28 Sept. 1419 (*Reg. Bubwith* II 375). D. before 4 Sept. 1426 (*Reg. Stafford* (*Bath and Wells*) I 41).

M. **John Hody** B.C.L. 1426–1440.
Coll. 4 Sept. 1426 (*Reg. Stafford* (*Bath and Wells*) I 41). D. before 19 March 1440 (*ibid.* II 247).

M. **John Storthwayt** B.Cn. & C.L. 1440–1452.
Coll. 19 March 1440 (*Reg. Stafford* (*Bath and Wells*) II 247). D. before 2 Feb. 1452 (*Reg. Bekynton* I 177).

M. **Thomas Chaundeler** B.Th. 1452–1467.
Coll. 14 July 1452 (*Reg. Bekynton* I 186). Exch. chancellorship with John Morer for ch. of All Hallows the Great, London, 18 Dec. 1467 (Lond., Guildhall, Reg. T. Kempe pt.i f. 110b).

M. **John Morer** D.M. 1467–?
By exch. Dec. 1467.

M. **Thomas Overary** B.C.L. ?–1472.
Occ. 11 Feb. 1469 (*CPL.* XII 636). Precentor 1472.

M. **Robert Wilson** D.C.L. 1472–1496.
Coll. 11 Aug. 1472 (*Reg. Stillington* p. 95). D. before 14 Sept. 1496 (*Cal. MSS. D. & C. Wells* II 145).

M. **Walter Felde** D.Th. 1496–1499.
Adm. 14 Sept. 1496 (*Cal. MSS. D. & C. Wells* II 145). D. before 15 Apr. 1499 (*Reg. King* p. 29).

M. **Thomas Cornish** M.A., O.St.J. of Jer. Bp. of Tine. 1499–1502.
Coll. 17 Apr. 1499 (*Reg. King* p. 29). Adm. 21 Apr. (*Cal. MSS. D. & C. Wells* II 155). Precentor 1502.

M. **John Pikman** D.Cn.L. 1502–1503.
Adm. 4 Sept. 1502 (*Cal. MSS. D. & C. Wells* II 167). D. 6 Feb./15 March 1503 (*Som. Med. Wills 1501–1530* p. 39).

M. **Alexander Hody** B.Cn.L. 1503–1504.
Adm. 14 Aug. 1503 (*Cal. MSS. D. & C. Wells* II 171). Res. before 1 Apr. 1504 (*CPR. 1494–1509* p. 347).

M. **Robert Dyker** B.Cn. & C.L. 1504–?
Royal gr. 1 Apr. 1504 (*CPR. 1494–1509* p. 347). Occ. 11 Jan. 1516 (*Reg. King* p. 180).

M. **James Fitzjames** D.Th. 1522.
Occ. 5 Sept. 1522 (*Reg. Bps., 1518–1559* p. 35).

TREASURERS

John de Langeton ?–1305.
Occ. 28 Sept. 1294 (*CPR. 1292–1301* p. 95). Bp. of Chichester 1305.

Arnald son of Amaneuus de le Breto ?–1309.
Occ. 22 Feb. 1308 (*CPR. 1307–1313* p. 47). D. before 16 March 1309 (*CPL.* II 51).

Amaneuus de Astariaco 1309.
Occ. 23 June 1309 (*CPL.* II 60).

M. **Jordan de Moraunt** 1309–1319.
Royal gr. 19 Sept. 1309 (*CPR. 1307–1313* p. 191). Royal prohibn. to persons disturbing possession, 1 June 1310 (*ibid.* p. 229). Exch. treasurership with John de Bruton for ch. of Sawbridgeworth, Herts., 12 Feb. 1319 (*Reg. Drokensford* p. 21).

M. **John de Bruton** 1319–1320.
William de Clopton 1320.
Bruton obtained treasurership by exch. Feb. 1319. Res. c. 4 Apr. 1320 when negotiating exch. of treasurership for ch. of Tydd St Mary, Lincs. (Reg. Drokensford f. 134). Clopton prov. to treasurership, mand. adm. 4 May (Reg. 1 f. 152b). Bruton's exch. unsuccessful, tried to regain treasurership, but held by Clopton. Bruton complained to abp. 5 Aug. (*Reg. Drokensford* p. 144). Clopton cited 23 Aug. by abp. for unlawful possession and bp. ordered to reinstate Bruton (*ibid.*). Bruton made formal res. of treasurership 28 Oct. (*ibid.* p. 182). Clopton res. or depriv. s.d. (*ibid.* pp. 182–3).

M. **Richard de Forde** D.C.L. 1320–1327.
Coll. 28 Oct. 1320 (*Reg. Drokensford* pp. 182–3). D. before 28 Apr. 1327 (*ibid.* p. 267).

Richard de Thistleden 1327–1348.
Coll. 28 Apr. 1327 (*Reg. Drokensford* p. 267). D. 4 Nov. 1348 (*Reg. R. de Salopia* II 690).

M. **Richard de Tormeton** B.Cn. & C.L. 1348–1361.
Roger de Chestrefeld 1351–1352.
Tormeton adm. 27 Nov. 1348 (*Reg. R. de Salopia* II 690). Chestrefeld prov. 20 Apr. 1351 (*CPL.* III 414). Res. before 13 Nov. 1352 when petition to pope for conf. of coll. of Tormeton (*CPP.* I 237). Conf. of gr. 18 Jan. 1353 (*CPL.* III 514). D. before 4 July 1361 (*CPP.* I 370).

Peter Iterii de Perigueux Card. pr. of SS. Quattuor Coronati. 1361–1367.
Prov. 12 Nov. 1361 (*CPP.* I 323). D. 20 May 1367 (*Eubel* I 35).

Thomas de Brantyngham 1367–1370.
Mark de Viterbo O.F.M. Card. pr. of S. Praxedis. 1368.
Royal gr. to Brantyngham 19 July 1367 (*CPR. 1367–1370* p. 1). Viterbo commended to k. 29 Jan. 1368 (*CPL.* IV 26). Brantyngham bp. of Exeter 1370.

Thomas Lynton 1380.
Comm. by k. to arrest persons disturbing rights of Lynton to treasurership, 20 Aug. 1380 (*CPR. 1377–1381* p. 575).

M. **William Lambrok** 1386–1439.
Raynald de Brancacio Card. dcn. of SS. Vitus et Modestus. ?–1393.
Estate of Lambrok ratif. 29 Apr. 1386 (*CPR. 1385–1389* p. 137), and 15 July (*ibid.* p. 201). Royal gr. 7 Aug. (*ibid.* p. 199). Writ of prohibn. 6 March 1389 against

persons acting in prejudice of appointment of Lambrok (*Cal. MSS. D. & C. Wells* I 284). Treasurership claimed by de Brancacio n.d., litigation at curia where sentence given in his favour and perpetual silence imposed upon Lambrok (*CPL.* IV 468–9). Lambrok excomm. because refused to resign (*ibid.*). Reinstated by pope Boniface IX 5 July 1393 (*ibid.*). D. before 21 Apr. 1439 (*Reg. Stafford (Bath and Wells)* II 236).

M. **Peter Stukeley** B.C.L. 1439–1451.
    Coll. 17 Sept. 1439 (*Reg. Stafford (Bath and Wells)* II 236). D. before 3 May 1451 (*Reg. Bekynton* I 160).

M. **John Bernard** B.Cn.L. 1451–1460.
    Coll. 3 May 1451 (*Reg. Bekynton* I 160). D. before 30 Apr. 1460 (*ibid.* p. 343).

M. **Hugh Sugar** *or* **Norris** D.C.L. 1460–1489.
    Coll. 1 May 1460 (*Reg. Bekynton* I 343). D. before 5 May 1489 (PCC 23 Milles).

M. **Thomas Harris** B.Cn.L. 1489–1511.
    Profession to bp. 18 Sept. 1489 (Liber Ruber f. 27). D. before 18 Feb. 1511 (*Cal. MSS. D. & C. Wells* II 226).

M. **John Chamber** D.M. 1511–1543.
    Adm. 18 Feb. 1511 (*Cal. MSS. D. & C. Wells* II 226). Res. before 15 May 1543 (*Reg. Bps., 1518–1559* p. 102).

SUBDEANS

William de la Forde de Yatton ?–1324.
    Occ. 28 Apr. 1314 (Reg. Drokensford f. 68). D. before 22 Jan. 1324 (*ibid.* ff. 217, 210).

M. **Walter Broun** B.C.L. 1324–1334.
    Coll. 4 Apr. 1324 (Reg. Drokensford f. 210). D. before 8 Nov. 1334 (*Reg. R. de Salopia* I 180).

M. **Walter de Burton** D.Th. 1334–1335.
    Coll. 8 Nov. 1334 (*Reg. R. de Salopia* I 180). D. or res. before 27 March 1335 (*ibid.* p. 189).

Walter de Hulle 1335–1342.
    Coll. 27 March 1335 (*Reg. R. de Salopia* I 189). Exch. subdeanery with Matthew de Valenciis for archdcnry of Bath, 29 Sept. 1342 (*ibid.* II 454).

Matthew de Valenciis 1342.
    By exch. Sept. 1342. Exch. subdeanery with William de Lavyngton for ch. of Langley Burrell, Wilts., 5 Dec. (*Reg. R. de Salopia* II 457).

William de Lavyngton 1342–?
    By exch. Dec. 1342. Occ. 21 March 1349 (*Reg. R. de Salopia* II 586).

John Auger ?–1350.
    Exch. subdeanery with William de Cammel for ch. of Yeovilton, Som., 18 July 1350 (*Reg. R. de Salopia* II 635–6).

William de Cammel 1350–1361.
    By exch. July 1350. Occ. 13 Oct. 1361 (*Cal. MSS. D. & C. Wells* I 264). Occ. as precentor in Dec.

Nicholas de Pontesbury 1366, 1369.
    Occ. Sept. 1366 (*Reg. Langham* p. 66). Occ. 5 Nov. 1369 (*Cal. MSS. D. & C. Wells* I 270).

M. **Thomas Byngham** M.Th. 1375, 1404.

M. **William Whyte** 1378.

Byngham occ. as subdean 1 and 13 Oct. 1375 (*Cal. MSS. D. & C. Wells* I 274, 275) and 1377 (P.R.O., E 179/4/1). Whyte occ. 7 Aug. 1378, then recently deceased (*CPL.* VII 55). Estate of Byngham ratif. 14 July 1390 (*CPR. 1388–1392* p. 298). Occ. 24 Dec. 1404 (*Reg. Giffard and Bowet* p. 54).

M. **Nicholas Mockyng** B.C.L. ?–1424.

Occ. 5 July 1406 (*CPL.* VI 92). D. before 16 Oct. 1424 (*Reg. Bubwith* II 459).

John Reynold 1424–1450.

Coll. 16 Oct. 1424 (*Reg. Bubwith* II 459). Estate ratif. 15 Nov. (*CPR. 1422–1429* p. 255). D. before 9 Apr. 1450 (*Reg. Bekynton* I 144).

M. **Thomas Boleyn** 1450–1451.

Coll. 20 Apr. 1450 (*Reg. Bekynton* I 146). Precentor 1451.

M. **John Spekyngton** M.A. 1451–1463.

Coll. 20 Nov. 1451 (*Reg. Bekynton* I 172–3). D. before 1 Jan. 1463 (*ibid.* p. 380).

M. **John Wansford** 1463–1491.

Coll. 1 Jan. 1463 (*Reg. Bekynton* I 380). Res. before 29 Sept. 1491 (*CPR. 1485–1494* p. 365).

M. **William Boket** D.Cn.L. 1491–1500.

Royal gr. 29 Sept. 1491 (*CPR. 1485–1494* p. 365). Adm. 4 Oct. (*Cal. MSS. D. & C. Wells* II 125). D. before 25 May 1500 (*Reg. King* p. 49).

M. **Robert Widewe** B.Mus. 1500–1505.

Coll. 25 May 1500 (*Reg. King* p. 49). D. before 5 Oct. 1505 (*Cal. MSS. D. & C. Wells* II 184).

John Hans 1505–1509.

Adm. 5 Oct. 1505 (*Cal. MSS. D. & C. Wells* II 184). D. before 8 Feb. 1509 (*ibid.* p. 211).

M. **Reginald West** 1509–1516.

Adm. 8 Feb. 1509 (*Cal. MSS. D. & C. Wells* II 211). D. 22 Feb./6 March 1516 (*Som. Med. Wills 1501–1530* pp. 183–6).

M. **Thomas Lovel** D.Cn.L. 1516–?

Occ. 7 May 1516 (*Reg. King* p. 181). Occ. 23 March 1522 (*Reg. Bps., 1518–1559* p. 25).[1]

M. **William Boureman** B.C.L. 1536, 1546.

Occ. 4 Aug. 1536 (*Som. Med. Wills 1531–1558* p. 30), May 1541 (Lamb., Reg. Cranmer f. 262) and 30 March 1546 (*Reg. Bps., 1518–1559* p. 114).

ARCHDEACONS OF WELLS

Note: The prebend of Huish and Brent was attached to the archdeaconry of Wells.

M. **Peter de Insula** *or* **Lisle** ?–1303.

Occ. 11 Dec. 1295 (*CPR. 1292–1301* p. 213). D. 24 Jan. 1303 (*Cal. MSS. D. & C. Wells* I 164).

---

[1] There is no evidence that James Fitzjames was subdean in 1524 as stated in Le Neve-Hardy.

Thomas de Charlton ?–1326.
Res. this archdcnry 24 May 1326 (*Reg. Drokensford* p. 24).

M. Wibert de Lutleton B.C.L. 1326.
Mand. adm. successor of Charlton 24 May 1326 (*Reg. Drokensford* p. 24). Lutleton exch. archdcnry with Robert de Wamberg for ch. of Market Lavington, Wilts., and preb. of Whitelackington, 13 June (*ibid.*).

Robert de Wamberg 1326–?
M. Simon de Montacute M.A. 1329–1332.
M. Thomas Upton 1330–?
Wamberg obtained archdcnry by exch. June 1326. Royal gr. to Montacute 29 June 1329 (*CPR. 1327–1330* p. 403). Montacute cited by abp. 15 Feb. 1330 because of unlawful claim to archdcnry (*Reg. R. de Salopia* I 33). K. had recovered pres. to archdcnry and had sent mand. adm. Montacute 12 Feb. (*ibid.*). Royal prohibn. to bp. 16 Feb. against collating to archdcnry (*ibid.*). Mand. to bp. 20 Feb. to adm. Montacute (*ibid.*). Bp. replied s.d. that unable to do this (*ibid.*). Royal gr. to Upton 15 Oct. (*CPR. 1330–1334* p. 9). Royal mand. adm. 24 Dec. (*ibid.* p. 30). Prohibns. 18 Apr. 1331 against all persons proceeding in defiance of royal gr. (*ibid.* p. 101). Royal writs 26 Oct. and 3 Nov. to arrest all persons impugning k's right to pres. to archdcnry (*ibid.* p. 367; *Reg. R. de Salopia* I 210). Litigation between Montacute and Wamberg, decision in favour of Wamberg 24 Dec. 1332 (*Reg. R. de Salopia* I 210). Wamberg re-adm. s.d. (*ibid.* p. 135).

Robert Mortimer 1334, 1336.
Occ. 27 Feb. 1334 and 20 March 1336 (*CCR. 1333–1337* pp. 298, 664).

Hugh 1344.
Occ. 18 July 1344 (*CPL.* III 266).

M. Thomas Fastolf D.C.L. ?–1352.
Occ. 16 Apr. 1346 (*CPL.* III 194). Prov. to archdcnry mentioned 17 Jan. 1347 (*CPP.* I 105). Bp. of St Davids 1352.

William de Court O.Cist. Card. bp. of Tusculum. 1353–1361.
Prov. 3 Jan. 1353 (*CPL.* III 475). D. 12 June 1361 (*Eubel* I 39).

Stephen Aubert Card. dcn. of S. Maria in Aquiro. 1361–1369.
Prov. 27 Oct. 1361 (*CPP.* I 321). Res. before 21 Feb. 1369 (*Cal. MSS. D. & C. Wells* I 270–1).

Simon Langham O.S.B. Card. pr. of S. Sixtus. 1369–1376.
Adm. 21 Feb. 1369 (*Cal. MSS. D. & C. Wells* I 270–1). D. 22 July 1376 (*Eubel* I 21).[1]

M. Andrew Baret D.C.L. 1385–?
John de Rypon 1386–?
John Beer 1388–?
Thomas Tuttebury 1391.
Estate of Baret ratif. 5 Nov. 1385 (*CPR. 1385–1389* p. 68). Royal gr. 23 July and 26 Nov. 1386 (*ibid.* pp. 201, 245). Royal gr. to Rypon 1 Dec. (*ibid.* p. 246). Estate of Baret ratif. 4 July 1388, notwithstanding any gr. to Rypon or other persons (*ibid.* p. 480). Royal gr. to Beer 13 Sept. (*ibid.* p. 508). Royal gr. to Tuttebury 6 June 1391 (*CPR. 1388–1392* p. 428), but estate of Rypon ratif. 26 July (*ibid.* p. 472).

---

[1] There is no evidence that a cardinal William held the archdcnry after the d. of Simon Langham in 1376 as stated by Le Neve-Hardy.

Nicholas Slake 1391–1398.

Royal gr. 28 Aug. and 1 Nov. 1391 (*CPR. 1388–1392* pp. 478, 492). Royal lic. 14 Apr. 1398 to accept prov. to archdcnry (*CPR. 1396–1399* p. 322). Exch. archdcnry with John Ikelyngton for ch. of St Mary Abchurch, London, 4 May (Lond., Guildhall, Reg. Braybroke ff. 159–159b).

John Ikelyngton 1398–1419.

By exch. May 1398. Estate ratif. 31 Oct. 1399 (*CPR. 1399–1401* p. 136). D. before 13 Apr. 1419 (*Reg. Bubwith* II 355).

M. Thomas Bubwith B.Cn. & C.L. 1419–1449.

Coll. 13 Apr. 1419 (*Reg. Bubwith* II 355). D. before 24 Oct. 1449 (*Reg. Bekynton* I 128).

M. Andrew Holes D.Cn.L. 1450–1470.

Coll. 15 Apr. 1450 (*Reg. Bekynton* I 145). Adm. 18 Apr. (*ibid.*). D. 1 Apr. 1470 (Salis., Machon, Chapter Act Book p. 36).[1]

Thomas Bridlington ?–1473.

Occ. 6 Aug. 1471 (*Reg. Stillington* p. 39). D. before 12 Apr. 1473 (*ibid.* p. 97).

M. William Nykke 1473–1494.

Coll. 12 Apr. 1473 (*Reg. Stillington* p. 96). Res. before 10 July 1494 (*ibid.* p. 192).

M. Richard Nix D.Cn. & C.L. 1494–1500.

Coll. 10 July 1494 (*Reg. Stillington* p. 192). Adm. 22 July (*Cal. MSS. D. & C. Wells* II 136). Bp. of Norwich 1500.[2]

M. Francis de Basleiden D.Cn.L Abp. of Besançon. 1500–1502.

Adm. 30 Dec. 1500 (*Cal. MSS. D. & C. Wells* II 161). Res. before 19 Nov. 1502 (*ibid.* p. 169).

M. Thomas Beaumont D.Cn. & C.L. 1502–1507.

Adm. 19 Nov. 1502 (*Cal. MSS. D. & C. Wells* II 169). D. 6 Feb./20 Nov. 1507 (*Som. Med. Wills 1501–1530* pp. 111–13).

M. Polydore Vergil or **Castellensis 1508–1546.**

Coll. 1 Jan. 1508 (*Reg. King* p. 127). Adm. by proxy 6 Feb. (*Cal. MSS. D. & C. Wells* II 207), in person 10 Sept. (*ibid.* p. 209). Res. archdcnry to k. 26 Dec. 1546 (*L. & P.* XXI ii No. 614).

ARCHDEACONS OF BATH

Henry de Sandwyco 1309–1333.

Royal gr. 8 Feb. 1309 (*CPR. 1307–1313* p. 100). D. before 5 July 1333 (*Reg. R. de Salopia* I 151).

Matthew de Valenciis 1333–1342.

Occ. 12 Sept. 1333 (*Reg. R. de Salopia* I 156). Suspended 17 Jan. 1341 and excomm. 17 July (*ibid.* p. 429), although bp. cited 14 July by official of ct. of Canterbury for preventing de Valenciis taking possession of archdcnry (*ibid.*). Exch. archdcnry with Walter de Hulle for subdeanery, 29 Sept. 1342 (*ibid.* II 454).

---

[1] There is no evidence that Richard Owen died in possession of the archdcnry in 1465 as stated by Le Neve-Hardy. Andrew Holes occ. as archdcn. in 1468 (*Reg. Stillington* p. 29), and appears to have held the archdcnry consistently from 1450 to 1470.

[2] Nix was prov. to the bpc. of Norwich in Feb. 1501, but since Thomas Jane, the previous bp., d. in Sept. 1500, Nix was probably el. bp. in that year. There is no account of his election.

Walter de Hulle 1342–1353.
By exch. Sept. 1342. D. before 7 March 1353 (*Reg. R. de Salopia* II 743).

John Power 1353–?
Coll. 7 March 1353 (*Reg. R. de Salopia* II 743). Occ. 18 Nov. 1366 (*Reg. Langham* p. 68).[1]

Hugh Herle 1380.
Occ. 28 June 1380 (*CPR. 1377–1381* p. 519).

Ranulf de Gorce de Monterac Card. pr. of S. Pudentiana. 1380.
Occ. 28 Aug. 1380 (*CPR. 1377–1381* p. 536).

M. **Roger Harewell** B.C.L. 1386–1428.
Royal gr. 23 July 1386 (*CPR. 1385–1389* p. 201). Estate ratif. 28 July (*ibid.* p. 208). Res. before 30 Jan. 1428 (*Reg. Stafford (Bath and Wells)* I 59).

M. **Thomas Warde** D.Cn.L. 1428–1449.
Coll. 30 Jan. 1428 (*Reg. Stafford (Bath and Wells)* I 59). Exch. archdcnry with William Sprever for ch. of Stone, Kent, 10 Dec. 1449 (*Reg. Bekynton* I 133).

M. **William Sprever** D.C.L. 1449–1460.
By exch. Dec. 1449. D. before 26 Feb. 1460 (*Reg. Bekynton* I 340).

M. **Hugh Sugar** *or* **Norris** D.C.L. 1460.
Coll. 26 Feb. 1460 (*Reg. Bekynton* I 340). Treasurer in May.

M. **Richard Lichefeld** D.C.L. 1460–1497.
Coll. 6 May 1460 (*Reg. Bekynton* I 344–5). D. before 17 March 1497 (*Cal. MSS. D. & C. Wells* II 146).

M. **William Cosyn** Lic.C.L. 1497–1498.
Coll. 17 March 1497 (*Cal. MSS. D. & C. Wells* II 146). Dean 1498.

M. **Thomas Beaumont** D.Cn. & C.L. 1499.
Adm. 31 March 1499 (*Cal. MSS. D. & C. Wells* II 155). Preb. of Combe Duodecima and provost in July.

M. **John Pikman** B.C.L. 1499–1502.
Coll. 12 July 1499 (*Reg. King* pp. 36–7). Adm. 21 July (*Cal. MSS. D. & C. Wells* II 156). Chancellor 1502.

M. **Thomas Tomyow** D.Cn. & C.L. 1502–1518.
Adm. 4 Sept. 1502 (*Cal. MSS. D. & C. Wells* II 167). D. before 12 Aug. 1518 (PCC 9 Ayloffe).

M. **Robert Shorton** D.Th. 1535.
Occ. 1535 (*Valor* I 133). D. 17 Oct. (Cambridge, Corpus Christi College, MS. 108 f. 90).

M. **Walter Cretynge** D.C.L. ?–1557.
Occ. 9 July 1540 (*L. & P.* xv No. 861). Occ. May 1541 (Lamb., Reg. Cranmer f. 264b). D. 2/20 Nov. 1557 (PCC 49 Wrastley; *Reg. Bps., 1518–1559* p. 149).

[1] There is no indication that Peter de Luna, 'card. of Aragon', held the archdcnry in 1376, as stated by Le Neve-Hardy.

ARCHDEACONS OF TAUNTON

Note: The prebend of Milverton Prima was attached to the archdeaconry of Taunton.

M. William de Molendino 1298–?
Adm. 16 Dec. 1298 by proxy (*Cal. MSS. D. & C. Wells* I 159). Adm. in person 1300 (*ibid.*)

M. Peter de Averburi 1302.
Occ. 13 Feb. and 3 July 1302 (*Cal. MSS. D. & C. Wells* I 159; *Reg. Winchelsey* I 441).

M. Henry de Schavington ?–1320.
Occ. 11 Dec. 1308 (*Reg. Winchelsey* II 1077). D. before 12 Dec. 1320 (*Reg. Drokensford* p. 184).

M. Robert Hereward 1320–?
Coll. 12 Dec. 1320 (*Reg. Drokensford* p. 184). Estate ratif. 10 Feb. 1332 (*CPR. 1330–1334* p. 249). Occ. 20 May 1351 (*CPL.* III 429). ? Held archdcnry until d. before 16 Apr. 1363 (*CPR. 1361–1364* p. 323).

M. William Thingull D.Cn. & C.L. 1364, 1366.
Occ. 18 June 1364, when gr. royal protection because unable to execute prov. to archdcnry (*CPR. 1364–1367* pp. 7–8). Occ. 18 Sept. 1366 (*Reg. Langham* p. 49).

Thomas Arundell 1370–1373.
Royal gr. 16 July 1370 (*CPR. 1367–1370* p. 456). Bp. of Ely 1373.

William de Aigrefeuille Card. pr. of S. Stephanus in Coelio monte. 1373.
Occ. 24 Sept. 1373 (*CPL.* IV 187).

Piero Tomacelli of Naples Card. dcn. of S. Georgius ad velum aureum. ?–1389.
Occ. 26 Feb. 1383 (*CPR. 1381–1385* p. 230). El. pope, Boniface IX, 1389.

Thomas Marton 1390–?
Royal gr. 12 Apr. 1390 (*CPR. 1388–1392* p. 241).

M. Ralph Erghum 1391.
Occ. 14 June 1391 (*Cal. MSS. D. & C. Wells* I 408).

M. Thomas Polton B.C.L. ?–1416.
M. Thomas Sparkeford B.C.L. 1395–1396.
William Elleford 1400.
Estate of Polton ratif. 3 May 1395 (*CPR. 1391–1396* p. 563). Royal gr. to Sparkeford 7 June (*ibid.* pp. 572–3). Probably res. 1396 when bp. of Waterford and Lismore, Ireland. Polton occ. as archdcn. 28 Apr. 1399 and 13 Apr. 1400 (*CPL.* V 248, 304). Royal gr. to Elleford 24 May (*CPR. 1399–1401* p. 295). Does not appear to have gained possession, since Polton occ. as archdcn. 19 Jan. 1401 (*CPL.* V 331). Exch. archdcnry with Nicholas Carlton for preb. of Compton Bishop, 1 Sept. 1416 (*Reg. Bubwith* I 243–4).

Nicholas Carlton 1416–1441.
By exch. Sept. 1416. D. before 1 Jan. 1441 (*Reg. Stafford (Bath and Wells)* II 260).

M. Adam Moleyns D.C.L. 1441–1445.
Coll. 1 Jan. 1441 (*Reg. Stafford (Bath and Wells)* II 260). Bp. of Chichester 1445.

M. **Andrew Holes** D.Cn.L. 1446–1450.
 Coll. 13 Feb. 1446 (*Reg. Bekynton* I 58). Archdcn. of Wells 1450.

M. **Robert Stillington** D.C.L. 1450–1465.
 Coll. 20 Apr. 1450 (*Reg. Bekynton* I 145). Bp. of Bath and Wells 1465.

 Richard Langport B.C.L. ?–1490.
 Occ. 20 May 1481 (*Reg. T. Bourgchier*, ed. F. R. H. Du Boulay (Canterbury and York Soc., liv) p. 147). D. 20 June/12 July 1490 (PCC 27 Milles; *Cal. MSS. D. & C. Wells* II 119).

M. **Oliver King** D.Cn. & C.L. 1490–1492.
 Adm. 12 July 1490 (*Cal. MSS. D. & C. Wells* II 119). Bp. of Exeter 1492.

M. **William Worsley** D.C.L. 1493–1496.
 Coll. 18 Feb. 1493 (*Reg. Stillington* p. 179). Res. before 16 Dec. 1496 (*Reg. King* p. 2).

M. **Robert Sherburn** M.A., B.M. 1496–1505.
 Coll. 16 Dec. 1496 (*Reg. King* p. 2). Bp. of St Davids 1505.

M. **John Ednam** D.Th. 1505–1509.
 Adm. 27 May 1505 (*Cal. MSS. D. & C. Wells* II 182). Res. before 18 Aug. 1509 (*ibid.* p. 214).

M. **Robert Honywode** D.C.L. 1509–1522/3.
 Adm. 18 Aug. 1509 (*Cal. MSS. D. & C. Wells* II 214). D. 25 Dec. 1522/26 Feb. 1523 (PCC 2 Bodfelde).

 John Monyns ?–1525.
 Occ. 17 Oct. 1524 (*Som. Med. Wills 1501–1530* p. 230). D. 3 Apr./9 Oct. 1525 (PCC 37 Bodfelde).

M. **Stephen Gardiner** D.Cn. & C.L. 1526, 1529.
 Occ. 8 Feb. 1526 (*L. & P.* IV i No. 1926 p. 886). Occ. 1529 (*ibid.* IV iii No. 6047 p. 2698). ? Held archdcnry until bp. of Winchester 1531.

M. **Thomas Cranmer** D.Th. ?–1533.
 Archdcn. until abp. of Canterbury, Feb. 1533. Called late archdcn. of Taunton in May (*L. & P.* VI No. 578 (8)).

M. **Roland Lee** D.Cn.L. 1533–1534.
 Occ. 10 Sept. 1533 (*L. & P.* VI No. 1109). Bp. of Coventry and Lichfield 1534.

M. **Richard Sampson** D.C.L. 1535.
 Occ. 1535 (*Valor* I 132).

M. **George Henneage** B.Cn.L. 1540.
 Occ. 11 June and 9 July 1540 (*L. & P.* xv Nos. 772 and 861).

M. **John Dakyn** D.C.L. ?–1541.
 Res. this archdcnry 24 Oct. 1541 (*L. & P.* XVIII i No. 66 (30)).

M. **John Redmayn** D.Th. 1541–1558.
 Accepted archdcnry 24 Oct. 1541 (*L. & P.* XVIII i No. 66 (30)). Conf. by Parliament 21 Jan. 1542 (*ibid.*). D. before 27 Jan. 1558 (PCC 3 Noodes).

PREBENDARIES OF ASHILL

Henry de Scales ?–1311.
Res. this preb. before 6 Jan. 1311 (*Reg. Drokensford* p. 60).

C

Richard de Drokensford 1311–1316.
M. Thomas de Wilton B.Th. 1311–?
Hamelin de Godelee 1316–?
Drokensford coll. 6 Jan. 1311 (*Reg. Drokensford* p. 60). Wilton prov. 2 March (*CPL.* II 82). Drokensford d. before 9 Sept. 1316, then called preb. of Ashill (*Reg. Drokensford* p. 109). Godelee coll. 12 Sept. (*ibid.* p. 112). Wilton occ. as preb. of Ashill June 1317 (*CPL.* II 153). Occ. as preb. of Wells 9 Oct. 1322 (*ibid.* p. 225).

M. Roger de Nassington ?–1364.
Prov. to canonry at Wells with expectation of preb. 21 Jan. 1322 (*CPL.* II 225). Occ. as preb. of Ashill 16 Oct. 1333 (*Reg. R. de Salopia* I 157). D. before 1 March 1364 (*CPR. 1361–1364* p. 480).

John de Saunford 1364–?
Royal gr. 1 March 1364 (*CPR. 1361–1364* p. 480). Occ. 17 Oct. 1366 (*Reg. Sudbury* II 170).

William Chaumbre ?–1391/2.
M. William Lambrok 1386.
Chaumbre occ. 22 Feb. 1379 (*Cal. MSS. D. & C. Wells* I 283). Royal gr. to Lambrok 11 Aug. 1386 (*CPR. 1385–1389* p. 202). Estate of Chaumbre ratif. 13 Nov. (*ibid.* p. 238). D. as preb. Sept. 1391/2 (*Cal. MSS. D. & C. Wells* II 22).

M. Richard Bruton ?–1417.
Occ. 1391/2 (*Cal. MSS. D. & C. Wells* II 22). Estate ratif. 4 Aug. 1394 (*CPR. 1391–1396* p. 470). D. 30 Oct./20 Nov. 1417 (PCC 39 Marche; *Reg. Bubwith* I 293, 297).

John Roland 1417–1426.
Coll. 26 Dec. 1417 (*Reg. Bubwith* I 297). D. before 12 July 1426 (*Reg. Stafford (Bath and Wells)* I 40).

John Hillier 1426–1433.
Coll. 12 July 1426 (*Reg. Stafford (Bath and Wells)* I 40). Preb. of St Decumans 1433.

M. David Price D.C.L. 1433–1434.
Coll. 10 Nov. 1433 (*Reg. Stafford (Bath and Wells)* II 153). Res. before 20 June 1434 (*ibid.* p. 164).

M. Richard Moresby B.Cn. & C.L. 1434–1445.
Coll. 20 June 1434 (*Reg. Stafford (Bath and Wells)* II 164). Res. before 5 Dec. 1445 (*Reg. Bekynton* I 53).

M. John Sperkhauke D.Th. 1445–1474.
Coll. 5 Dec. 1445 (*Reg. Bekynton* I 53). D. before 20 Dec. 1474 (*Reg. Stillington* p. 103).

M. John Wansford 1474–1493.
Coll. 20 Dec. 1474 (*Reg. Stillington* p. 103). D. before 3 Feb. 1493 (*Som. Med. Wills 1383–1500* pp. 297–8).

M. Ralph Lepton B.C.L. 1493–?
Coll. 12 Apr. 1493 (*Reg. Stillington* p. 180). Occ. 13 June 1504 (*Reg. King* p. 95).

M. Robert Bisse D.Cn. & C.L. 1535, 1541.
Occ. 1535 (*Valor* I 135). Occ. May 1541 (Lamb., Reg. Cranmer f. 254b). ? Held preb. until d. before 20 Dec. 1546 (Salis., Reg. Capon f. 32b).

PREBENDARIES OF BARTON ST DAVID

William de Carleton ?–1311.
D. as preb. before 3 March 1311 (Reg. Drokensford f. 35).

M. John de Winchelsey M.A. 1311–1323.
Coll. 11 March 1311 (Reg. Drokensford f. 25). Res. by proxy 24 March 1323, formal res. in person 31 March (*Reg. Drokensford* p. 215).

M. Robert de Baldock *junior* D.C.L. 1323–1353.
Peter de Nantolio 1326.
Baldock coll. 31 March 1323 (*Reg. Drokensford* p. 215). Mand. adm. Nantolio 13 June 1326, exch. had been arranged between Nantolio and Baldock, preb. of Barton St David for preb. in Ripon colleg. ch., Yorks. (*ibid.*). Nantolio res. Barton St David before 31 Aug.—the exch. had evidently been ineffective—Baldock re-adm. (*ibid.* p. 263). D. before 21 Jan. 1353 (*Reg. R. de Salopia* ii 707–8).

M. Thomas de Bukton D.C.L. 1353–1363.
Coll. 21 Jan. 1353 (*Reg. R. de Salopia* ii 707–8). Preb. of Shalford 1363.

M. Thomas Bray M.A. 1366.
Occ. 19 Sept. 1366 (*Reg. Langham* p. 75).

William Colvyle 1372.
Occ. 27 Feb. 1372 (*Cal. MSS. D. & C. Wells* i 488).

Robert de Stonore ?–1381/2.
D. as preb. 17 Dec. 1381/Sept. 1382 (*Reg. Gilbert* p. 123; *Cal. MSS. D. & C. Wells* ii 17).

John de Lincoln 1397, 1399.
Estate ratif. 25 May 1397 (*CPR. 1396–1399* p. 139) and 22 Oct. 1399 (*CPR. 1399–1401* p. 24).

M. Walter de Medeford B.C.L. 1404–1413.
Adm. 31 Aug. 1404 (*Reg. Giffard and Bowet* p. 52). Dean 1413.

M. John Stafford D.C.L. 1413–1423.
Coll. 11 Nov. 1413 (*Reg. Bubwith* i 165). Dean 1423.

John Shelford 1423–1473/4.
Coll. 10 Sept. 1423 (*Reg. Bubwith* ii 443). D. Sept. 1473/4[1] (*Cal. MSS. D. & C. Wells* ii 96).

M. John Staunton M.A. 1472–?
Coll. 11 March 1472 (*Reg. Stillington* p. 95).

M. John Hill ?–1494.
D. as preb. before 1 Feb. 1494 (*Reg. Stillington* p. 190).

M. William Thompson B.Th. 1494–1497.
Coll. 1 Feb. 1494 (*Reg. Stillington* p. 190). Adm. 31 March (*Cal. MSS. D. & C. Wells* ii 135). Res. before 6 Apr. 1497 (*ibid.* p. 146).

[1] Shelford's d. is reported in the Michaelmas accounts of the dean and chapter of Wells which are apparently inaccurate on occasions. This is explained by the 'ancient custom' that the income of prebends vacant by death was payable to the escheator, a cathedral official, for the first year after the occurrence of the vacancy (*Cal. MSS. D. & C. Wells* ii p. x).

M. William Fitzherbert D.Cn.L. 1497-?
    Adm. 6 Apr. 1497 (*Cal. MSS. D. & C. Wells* II 146). ? Held preb. until d. before May 1514 (*Emden, Reg. Ox.* II 689).

M. William Boureman B.C.L. 1523, 1535.
    Occ. 24 March 1523 (*Reg. Bps., 1518-1559* p. 25). Occ. 15 Nov. 1535 (*L. & P.* IX No. 823).

Richard Eryngton 1535.
    Occ. 1535 (*Valor* I 135).

PREBENDARIES OF BUCKLAND DINHAM

Walter de Clipston ?-1310.
    D. as preb. before 31 Dec. 1310 (*Reg. Drokensford* p. 37).

Robert de Clipston 1310-?
Richard de Clipston 1316-?
    Robert coll. 31 Dec. 1310 (*Reg. Drokensford* p. 37). Richard coll. 3 May 1316 (*ibid.* p. 106), but the bp's letter about coll. has date 1 Feb. 1311 but not sealed until 1316. Possibly confusion has occurred with the Christian names Robert and Richard, as Robert occ. as preb. 13 Oct. 1329 (*Reg. R. de Salopia* I 8) and 29 March 1348 (*ibid.* II 581).

Walter de Byrecombe 1360.
    Occ. 27 Oct. 1360 (*Reg. R. de Salopia* II 773).

John de Newenham 1363-1365.
    Royal gr. 1 Oct. 1363 (*CPR. 1361-1364* p. 387). Exch. preb. with Richard de Boule for preb. in St John's colleg. ch., Chester, 27 Jan. 1365 (*1st and 2nd Reg. of Bishop R. de Stretton*, ed. R. A. Wilson (William Salt Archaeol. Soc., 1905-7) II 165-6).

M. Richard de Boule B.C.L. 1365-?
    By exch. Jan. 1365. Occ. 16 Oct. 1366 (*Reg. Langham* p. 93).

Thomas Alston 1379.
    Occ. 22 Feb. 1379 (*Cal. MSS. D. & C. Wells* I 283).

M. Gilbert Stone ?-1401.
    Estate ratif. 18 Feb. 1394 (*CPR. 1391-1396* p. 373). Res. before 22 Nov. 1401 (*Reg. Giffard and Bowet* p. 15).

Thomas Terry ?-1409.
    D. as preb. before 23 Jan. 1409 (*Reg. Bubwith* I 49).

M. Thomas Bubwith 1409-1410.
    Coll. 23 Jan. 1409 (*Reg. Bubwith* I 49). Preb. of St Decumans 1410.

John Roland 1410-1417.
    Coll. 9 Apr. 1410 (*Reg. Bubwith* I 75). Preb. of Ashill 1417.

John Knyght 1417-1425.
    Coll. 27 Dec. 1417 (*Reg. Bubwith* I 297). D. before 8 Sept. 1425 (*Reg. Stafford (Bath and Wells)* I 31).

Richard Cawdray 1425-1431.
    Coll. 8 Sept. 1425 (*Reg. Stafford (Bath and Wells)* I 31). Res. before 23 Oct. 1431 (*ibid.* p. 115).

William Gray[1] 1431–?
Coll. 23 Oct. 1431 (*Reg. Stafford (Bath and Wells)* I 115).

M. Oliver Dynham M.A. 1454–1479.
Coll. 14 Sept. 1454 (*Reg. Bekynton* I 236). Res. before 8 Feb. 1479 (*Reg. Stillington* p. 112).

M. Nicholas Goldwell B.C.L. 1479–1505.
Coll. 8 Feb. 1479 (*Reg. Stillington* p. 112). D. before Nov. 1505 (Norwich, Reg. Nix XIII f. 58).

M. Gundissalvus Ferdinandus 1506–1513.
Adm. 19 Apr. 1506 (*Cal. MSS. D. & C. Wells* II 193). D. before 31 July 1513 (*ibid.* p. 234).

M. Thomas Lovel D.Cn.L. 1513–?
Adm. 31 July 1513 (*Cal. MSS. D. & C. Wells* II 234). Occ. 20 Aug. 1514 (*Reg. King* p. 170).

M. Richard Duck D.Th. 1533, 1535.
Occ. 1533 (*Reg. Bps., 1518–1559* p. 61). Occ. 1535 (*Valor* I 135). ? Held preb. until d. by 2 Aug. 1539 (Salis., Reg. Capon f. 16).

PREBENDARIES OF CARHAMPTON

Note: This prebend was held by the priors of Bath.

Thomas de Winton O.S.B. 1290–1301.
Lic. el. gr. 14 Jan. 1290 (*Chartularies of Bath* II 84). Winton occ. as prior 21 Dec. (*ibid.* p. 91). Res. 10 Apr. 1301 (*ibid.* p. 134).

Robert de Clopcote O.S.B. 1301–1332.
Lic. el. gr. 11 Apr. 1301 (*Chartularies of Bath* II 112). El. of Clopcote 14 Apr. (*ibid.*). D. before 27 Feb. 1332 (*Reg. R. de Salopia* I 86).

Robert de Sutton O.S.B. 1332.
Thomas Crist O.S.B. 1332–1340.
Lic. el. sought 27 Feb. 1332 (*Reg. R. de Salopia* I 86). Gr. 28 Feb. (*ibid.*). Comm. by bp. to confirm el. of Sutton and install 11 March (*ibid.* p. 96). El. conf. 12 March (*ibid.* p. 93). Instal. 14 March (*Chartularies of Bath* II 134). Stated 6 Apr. that prov. had been made to priory (*ibid.* p. 135), but Sutton occ. as prior 30 Apr. (*ibid.* p. 137). Res. after 14 July when Crist prov. (*CPL.* II 357). Crist res. before 12 Aug. 1340 (*Reg. R. de Salopia* I 370).

John de Iforde O.S.B. 1340–?
Lic. el. sought 12 Aug. 1340 (*Reg. R. de Salopia* I 370). Iforde el., occ. as prior 7 Aug. 1346 (*ibid.* II 535). Occ. 8 June 1350 (*CPL.* III 368). Appears to have d. or res. before 31 July 1359 since pres. made to ch. of St Mary Bath by subprior that day— suggests that priorate then vac. (*Chartularies of Bath* II 181).

John de Berewyk O.S.B. 1377.
John prior of Bath occ. 20 June 1362 (*CPR. 1361–1364* p. 225). John de Berewyk prior occ. before June 1377[2] (P.R.O., E 179/4/2).

---

[1] William Gray may possibly be identified with William Gray bp. of Ely 1454–1478, since the next coll. to the preb. of Buckland Dinham was made in 1454, but the evidence is insufficient to establish this identification.

[2] He occurs in a clerical subsidy list, compiled 51 Edward III (25 Jan.–21 June 1377).

John Dunster O.S.B. ?–1412.

Said to have been prior in reign of Richard II, i.e. after June 1377 (*CPR. 1429–1436* p. 473). Occ. 3 May 1397 (*CPL.* v 50). D. 6 Feb. 1412 (*Reg. Bubwith* II 476).

John Telesford O.S.B. 1412–?

Lic. el. sought 9 Feb. 1412 (*Reg. Bubwith* II 475). Gr. 13 Feb. (*ibid.*). El. 10 March (*ibid.* p. 476). Petition to bp. 14 March to confirm el. (*ibid.*). Opposers to el. cited to appear 23 March (*ibid.* p. 477). Mand. to install s.d. (*ibid.* p. 479). Occ. 26 Dec. 1424 (*CPR. 1422–1429* p. 265).

William Southbroke O.S.B. ?–1447.

Occ. 20 Apr. 1426 (*Reg. Stafford (Bath and Wells)* I 37–9). D. 7 June 1447 (*Reg. Bekynton* II 435).

Thomas Lacock O.S.B. 1447–?

Lic. el. sought 12 June 1447 (*Reg. Bekynton* II 435). Gr. 16 June (*ibid.*). El. 5 July, but chapt. agreed to delegate el. to bp. (*ibid.* p. 436). El. of Lacock in bp's presence 16 Sept. (*ibid.* p. 437). Conf. by bp. 25 Sept. (*ibid.*). Mand. to install s.d. (*ibid.*). Occ. 9 Oct. 1467 (*CPR. 1467–1477* p. 10).

John Dunster O.S.B. ?–1480/2.

John prior of Bath occ. 18 Feb. 1468 (*CPR. 1467–1477* p. 65). Prov. of Dunster to St Augustine's abbey, Canterbury, 13 Aug. 1480 (*CPL.* XIII i 5). Instructed to resign priorate of Bath, but called prior of Bath 16 June 1481 when received royal pardon for acceptance of papal bulls and gr. lic. to accept (*CPR. 1476–1485* p. 278). Royal assent to el. as abbot of St Augustine's 29 July 1482 (*ibid.* p. 310). Prov. again 27 Nov. (*CPL.* XIII ii 812–13)—then called monk of St Augustine's, not prior of Bath.

Peter O.S.B. 1482.

Occ. 13 Oct. and 7 Nov. 1482 (*CPR. 1476–1485* p. 278).

John Cantlow O.S.B. ?–1499.

Occ. 6 Nov. 1489 (*Reg. Stillington* p. 192). D. before 30 Aug. 1499 (*Reg. King* p. 87).

William Byrde O.S.B. 1499–1525.

Appointed by bp. 30 Aug. 1499 (*Reg. King* p. 87). He had been previously el. by priory, petition n.d. by subprior to bp. to release Byrde from excomm. or to gr. new lic. el. (*ibid.*). D. 22 May 1525 (*Reg. Bps., 1518–1559* p. 80).

William Holloway O.S.B. 1525–1539.

Lic. el. gr. 23 June 1525 (*Reg. Bps., 1518–1559* p. 80). El. 5 July (*ibid.* p. 81). Conf. by card. abp. of York 17 July (*ibid.*). Prior at surrender of Bath priory 27 Jan. 1539 (*L. & P.* XIV i No. 148).

PREBENDARIES OF CLEEVE

The abbots of Cleeve have not been included because they were not considered as members of the chapter at Wells. The prebend of Cleeve had been granted by bishop Savaric (1191–1205) to the abbot of Bec, and his community given full fraternity in the church of Wells (*Documents of the English lands of the abbey of Bec*, ed. M. Chibnall (Camden Soc., 3rd ser. lxxiii, 1951) pp. 4–5). In 1199 the monks of Bec agreed to lease the church of Cleeve to the abbot and monks of Cleeve for the sum of 44 marks annually. A list of the abbots of Cleeve is given in *VCH. Somerset* II 118. A list of the abbots of Bec is given in *Gallia Christiana* XI 231.

PREBENDARIES OF COMBE PRIMA

Henry de Carleton 1343.
Occ. 17 July 1343 (*Reg. R. de Salopia* II 466).

M. John Corf ?–1368.
Occ. 17 Oct. 1366 (*Reg. Langham* p. 27). Exch. preb. with Nicholas de Nyweton for preb. of Ruscombe Southbury, Salis., 19 May 1368 (*CPR. 1367–1370* pp. 110–11).

M. Nicholas de Nyweton B.Cn.L. 1368–?
By exch. May 1368.

Thomas de Orgrave ?–1377.
Exch. preb. and archdcnry of Cornwall with Robert de Braybroke for preb. of Fridaythorpe, York, 3 March 1377 (York, Reg. A. Neville I f. 5b).

M. Robert de Braybroke B.C.L. 1377–?
By exch. March 1377.

William Borstal ?–1381.
Occ. 22 Feb. and 4 March 1379 (*Cal. MSS. D. & C. Wells* I 283, 284). Exch. preb. with Nicholas de Braybroke for preb. of Funtington in Bosham royal free chap., Suss., 23 Nov. 1381 (Exeter, Reg. Brantyngham II f. 69).

M. Nicholas de Braybroke 1381–1382.
By exch. Nov. 1381. Mand. adm. 30 Nov. (Exeter, Reg. Brantyngham II f. 69). Adm. 5 Dec. (*ibid.*). Exch. preb. with John de Middleton for free chap. of St Margaret, Chelmsford, Essex, 11 July 1382 (Lond., Guildhall, Reg. Braybroke f. 11).

John de Middleton 1382–?
By exch. July 1382. Adm. 22 May (*sic*) (*Cal. MSS. D. & C. Wells* I 291).

William Ryell 1389–?
Royal gr. 9 Aug. 1389 (*CPR. 1388–1392* p. 97).

M. Hugh Hyckelyng ?–1413.
Exch. preb. with Reynold Bryte for preb. in Crediton colleg. ch., Devon, 18 Sept. 1413 (*Reg. Bubwith* I 148).

Reynold Bryte 1413–1434.
By exch. Sept. 1413. D. before 17 July 1434 (*Reg. Stafford (Bath and Wells)* II 165).

M. John Obezis D.Cn.L. 1434–1449.
Coll. 17 July 1434 (*Reg. Stafford (Bath and Wells)* II 165). D. before 16 July 1449 (*Reg. Bekynton* I 114).

M. John Wygrome M.A. 1449–1468/70.
Coll. 16 July 1449 (*Reg. Bekynton* I 114). Profession to bp. 26 July (*ibid.*). D. 1468/1470 (*Cal. MSS. D. & C. Wells* II 92).

M. John Morer D.M. ?–1472.
D. as preb. before 12 Jan. 1472 (*Reg. Stillington* p. 90).

Ralph Bury 1472–?
Coll. 24 Feb. 1472 (*Reg. Stillington* p. 91).

M. Christopher Twynyoo ?–1510.
Occ. as can. of Wells 26 June 1490 (*Reg. Stillington* p. 163). D. as preb. of Combe Prima before 1 Jan. 1510 (*Cal. MSS. D. & C. Wells* II 219).

William Wykes 1510–?

Adm. 1 Jan. 1510 (*Cal. MSS. D. & C. Wells* II 219).

John Eye 1535.

Occ. 1535 (*Valor* I 135). Occ. as preb. of Wells May 1541 (Lamb., Reg. Cranmer f. 262).

PREBENDARIES OF COMBE SECUNDA

M. John de Everdon ?–1335.

Occ. as preb. of Wells 18 May 1308 (*CPL.* II 42). D. as preb. of Combe Secunda before 24 July 1335 (*Reg. R. de Salopia* I 245–6).

Walter de Hulle 1335–1353.

Coll. 23 Aug. 1335 (*Reg. R. de Salopia* I 197). D. before 7 March 1353 (*ibid.* II 743).

John Power 1353–1361.

Coll. 7 March 1353 (*Reg. R. de Salopia* II 743). Preb. of Dultingcote 1361.

Robert atte Sloo 1366, 1379.

Occ. Oct. 1366 (*Reg. Langham* p. 39). Occ. 4 March 1379 (*Cal. MSS. D. & C. Wells* I 282). Occ. as can. 10 Jan. 1388 (Worcester, Reg. Wakefield f. 50).

M. Richard Stourton Sch.Th. ?–1437.

Occ. as can. of Wells Apr. 1410 (*Reg. Bubwith* II 468). D. before 13 July 1437, as preb. of Combe Secunda (*Reg. Stafford (Bath and Wells)* II 207–8).

Walter Foolde 1437–?

Coll. 13 July 1437 (*Reg. Stafford (Bath and Wells)* II 207–8).

M. Robert Widewe B.Mus. 1497–1500.

Adm. 17 March 1497 (*Cal. MSS. D. & C. Wells* II 146). Preb. of Holcombe 1500.

M. John Argentyne D.Th., D.M. 1500–1508.

Coll. 25 May 1500 (*Reg. King* p. 49). D. before 28 Apr. 1508 (*Cal. MSS. D. & C. Wells* II 207).

M. William Mors D.C.L. 1508–1519.

Adm. 28 Apr. 1508 (*Cal. MSS. D. & C. Wells* II 207). D. before 30 Nov. 1519 (*Reg. Bps., 1518–1559* p. 11).

M. William Capon D.Th. 1535.

Occ. 1535 (*Valor* I 136). ? Held preb. until d. before 28 Feb. 1550 (Lamb., Reg. Cranmer f. 107).

PREBENDARIES OF COMBE TERCIA

William de Estdene ?–1313.

Res. this preb. before 4 Apr. 1313 (Reg. Drokensford f. 138b).

M. William de Estdene 1313–1319.

Coll. 4 Apr. 1313 (Reg. Drokensford f. 138b). Exch. preb. with Matthew Husee for ch. of Pulborough, Suss., 12 March 1319 (*ibid.* f. 22b).

Matthew Husee 1319–1324.

By exch. March 1319. Exch. preb. and ch. of Yarlington, Som., with William de Pencriz for ch. of Bladon, Oxon., 9 Apr. 1324 (Reg. Drokensford f. 219).

William de Pencriz 1324–?

By exch. Apr. 1324.

M. **John de Sutton** 1341–?
   Matthew de Valenciis 1341.
   Sutton coll. 1 Jan. 1341 (*Reg. R. de Salopia* I 423). De Valenciis claimed preb. 30 March 1341 (*ibid.* II 445). Sutton probably retained possession since de Valenciis became subdean 1342.

   John Beneyt 1363.
   Occ. as preb. 31 Aug. 1363[1] when petitioned pope for conf. of coll. to preb. by bp. or fresh prov. to preb. if had been reserved (*CPP.* I 465).

   Robert Bays 1379.
   Occ. 4 March 1379 (*Cal. MSS. D. & C. Wells* I 284).

   William Excestre 1392–?
   Royal gr. 30 June 1392 (*CPR. 1391–1396* p. 119).

   Guy de Mona ?–1397.
   Res. this preb. 1397 when bp. of St Davids (*CPR. 1396–1399* p. 268).

   Walter Cook 1397–1399.
   Gr. royal lic. 5 Dec. 1397 to accept prov. (*CPR. 1396–1399* p. 268). Exch. preb. with Thomas Wybbe for free chap. of St Katherine, Chipping Campden, Glos., 20 Apr./12 May 1399 (Worcester, Reg. Tideman ff. 38–38b).

   Thomas Wybbe 1399–1409.
   By exch. Apr./May 1399. D. before 15 Dec. 1409 (*Reg. Bubwith* I 68).

   John Roland 1409–1410.
   Coll. 15 Dec. 1409 and 13 Jan. 1410 (*Reg. Bubwith* I 68, 2). Preb. of Buckland Dinham in Apr.

   Walter Shiryngton 1410–1417.
   Coll. 10 Apr. 1410 (*Reg. Bubwith* I 7). Exch. preb. with Thomas Pellican for preb. in Westbury-on-Trym colleg. ch., Glos., 8 Apr. 1417 (*ibid.* p. 279).

   Thomas Pellican 1417–1431.
   By exch. Apr. 1417. Adm. 14 May (*Reg. Bubwith* I 279). Exch. preb. with Richard Cordon for ch. of Shoreham, and chap. of Otford, Kent, 10 Nov. 1431 (*Reg. Stafford* (*Bath and Wells*) I 118).

M. **Richard Cordon** *or* **Broun** D.C.L. 1431–1453.
   By exch. Nov. 1431. D. before 5 Apr. 1453 (*Reg. Bekynton* I 203).

M. **John Pope** D.Th. 1453–1454.
   Coll. 5 Apr. 1453 (*Reg. Bekynton* I 203). Preb. of Henstridge 1454.

M. **John Spekyngton** M.A. 1454–1455.
   Coll. 30 Sept. 1454 (*Reg. Bekynton* I 239). Preb. of Easton in Gordano 1455.

M. **Henry Ergym** M.A. 1455–?
   Coll. 7 Nov. 1455 (*Reg. Bekynton* I 259). Occ., not called preb. of Combe Tercia, 29 Feb. 1464 (*ibid.* p. 410).

   Michael Cleve ?–1502.
   D. as preb. 29 Sept./23 Dec. 1502 (*Cal. MSS. D. & C. Wells* II 172, 169).

---

[1] Beneyt at this time held the preb. of Combe Terciadecima, occ. 1361 and 1366. There was possibly confusion at the papal chancery and the above confirmation should refer to his preb. of Combe Terciadecima not the preb. of Combe Tercia.

M. **Nicholas Halswell** D.M. 1502–?
Adm. 23 Dec. 1502 (*Cal. MSS. D. & C. Wells* II 169). ? Held preb. until d.
20 Jan./31 July 1528 (PCC 36 Porch).

William Crekynge 1535.
Occ. 1535 (*Valor* I 136).

PREBENDARIES OF COMBE QUARTA

M. **Robert de Cantuaria** 1322–?
Royal gr. 8 Oct. 1322 (*CPR. 1321–1324* p. 207).[1]

Robert de Stonore 1366.
Occ. Sept. 1366 (*Reg. Langham* p. 67).

M. **Thomas Bray** M.A. 1379.
Occ. as can. of Wells 1377 (P.R.O., E 179/4/1). Occ. as preb. of Combe Quarta
4 March 1379 (*Cal. MSS. D. & C. Wells* I 284). ? Held preb. until d. before 20 July
1383 (Exeter, Reg. Brantyngham I f. 108b).

M. **Adam Holme** ?–1399/1400.
D. as preb. Sept. 1399/1400 (*Cal. MSS. D. & C. Wells* II 33).

M. **Thomas Cosyn** ?–1413.
D. as preb. before 11 Aug. 1413 (*Reg. Bubwith* I 144).

M. **John Welles** 1413–1417.
Coll. 11 Aug. 1413 (*Reg. Bubwith* I 144). D. before 8 Nov. 1417 (*ibid.* p. 292).

M. **Thomas Stephens** Lic. C.L. 1417–1418.
Coll. 8 Nov. 1417 (*Reg. Bubwith* I 291–2). Preb. of Ilton 1418.

John Reynold 1418–1420.
Coll. 2 Nov. 1418 (*Reg. Bubwith* II 340). Preb. of Ilton 1420.

John Swyft 1420–1426.
Coll. 7 July 1420 (*Reg. Bubwith* II 392). Vac. preb. before 17 March 1426 (*Reg.
Stafford (Bath and Wells)* I 36).

M. **Thomas Circestre** B.Th. 1426–1453.
Coll. 17 March 1426 (*Reg. Stafford (Bath and Wells)* I 36). D. before 24 Feb. 1453
(*Reg. Bekynton* I 200).

Simon Belton 1453–1463.
Coll. 24 Feb. 1453 (*Reg. Bekynton* I 200). Exch. preb. with John Perche for preb.
of Carlton Paynell, Lincoln, 7 Apr. 1463 (*ibid.* p. 385).

M. **John Perche** B.M. 1463–1480/1.
By exch. Apr. 1463. D. as preb. Sept. 1480/1 (*Cal. MSS. D. & C. Wells* II 98).

M. **John Pikman** B.C.L. 1497–1499.
Adm. 20 March 1497 (*Cal. MSS. D. & C. Wells* II 146). Preb. of Ilton 1499.

M. **George Percy** B.Cn.L. 1499–1503.
Adm. 21 Apr. 1499 (*Cal. MSS. D. & C. Wells* II 155). Preb. of Ilton 1503.

M. **William Barons** D.C.L. 1503.
Adm. 27 May 1503 (*Cal. MSS. D. & C. Wells* II 171). Res. before 12 Nov. (*ibid.*
p. 174).

---

[1] John de Brabazon was coll. to this preb. 10 Nov. 1322, vac. by res. of William de Cherleton (Reg.
Drokensford f. 187), but the entry has been crossed out.

M. **Roger Churche** D.Cn.L. 1503–1524.
  Adm. 12 Nov. 1503 (*Cal. MSS. D. & C. Wells* II 174). D. 29 Sept./17 Oct. 1524 (*ibid.* p. 241; PCC 26 Bodfelde; *Reg. Bps., 1518–1559* p. 37).

M. **Edward Greye** 1524–1529/30.
  Coll. 8 Nov. 1524 (*Reg. Bps., 1518–1559* p. 37). Res. or depriv. Sept. 1529/30 (*Cal. MSS. D. & C. Wells* II 243).

M. **Thomas Bennet** D.C.L. 1535.
  Occ. 1535 (*Valor* I 136). ? Held preb. until d. 16 July/11 Sept. 1558 (PCC 45 Noodes).

PREBENDARIES OF COMBE QUINTA

Thomas de Stapleton 1327/8–1333.
  Adm. 1327/8 (*Cal. MSS. D. & C. Wells* II 4). Exch. preb. with William de Littleton for a preb. in St Probus colleg. ch., Cornw., 20 Aug./7 Sept. 1333 (Exeter, Reg. Grandisson II f. 167b; *Reg. R. de Salopia* I 152).

M. **William de Littleton** 1333–1355.
  By exch. Aug./Sept. 1333. D. before 30 Jan. 1355 (*CPP.* I 276).

M. **Edmund Gournay** Sch.C.L. 1355–1361.
  Prov. 30 Jan. 1355 (*CPP.* I 276). Preb. of Wormenstre 1361.

William de Cammel 1361–?
  Mand. adm. 23 Aug. 1361 (*Cal. MSS. D. & C. Wells* I 263). ? Res. before 18 Dec. when occ. as precentor.

M. **Thomas Young** Lic.Cn. & C.L. 1366.
  Occ. as can. of Wells 21 Aug. 1363 (*CPP.* I 451). Occ. as preb. of Combe Quinta 17 Oct. 1366 (*Reg. Sudbury* II 177–8). ? Held preb. until d. before 23 May 1377 (Lamb., Reg. Sudbury ff. 97–97b).

Roger Payn 1379.
  Occ. 22 Feb. 1379 (*Cal. MSS. D. & C. Wells* I 283).

John Mackworth ?–1406.
  Exch. preb. with John Prophete for preb. of Yatton, 23 Aug. 1406 (*Reg. Giffard and Bowet* p. 60).

M. **John Prophete** 1406.
  By exch. Aug. 1406. Exch. preb. with Richard Hull for St Radegund's free chap., St Paul's, London, 27 Nov. (*Reg. Giffard and Bowet* p. 66).

Richard Hull 1406–1408.
  By exch. Nov. 1406. Exch. preb. with John Hody for ch. of Wootton Courtney, Som., 31 Jan. 1408 (*Reg. Giffard and Bowet* p. 72).

M. **John Hody** B.C.L. 1408–1417.
  By exch. Jan. 1408. Adm. 6 Feb. (*Reg. Giffard and Bowet* p. 73). Preb. of Compton Bishop 1417.

M. **Thomas Frome** B.C.L. 1418–1424.
  Coll. 10 Jan. 1418 (*Reg. Bubwith* I 298). D. 2/28 Aug. 1424 (*ibid.* II 455–7).

William Toby 1424–?
  Coll. 13 Oct. 1424 (*Reg. Bubwith* II 450).

M. **William Toly** ?–1460.
> D. as preb. before 31 Oct. 1460 (*Reg. Bekynton* I 351).

M. **Thomas Hope** D.C.L. 1460–1488.
> Coll. 10 Nov. 1460 (*Reg. Bekynton* I 351). D. 21 Feb./11 March 1488 (PCC 5 Milles).

William Cockes 1488–?
> Adm. 5 May 1488 (*Cal. MSS. D. & C. Wells* II 111).

William Highwey 1500–?
> Adm. 20 Sept. 1500 (*Cal. MSS. D. & C. Wells* II 159). Occ. 1535 (*Valor* I 136).

PREBENDARIES OF COMBE SEXTA

Stephen Trippe 1342–?
> Coll. 12 May 1342 (*Reg. R. de Salopia* II 447).

John Brampton 1379, 1402/3.
M. **John Langton** Sch.Cn.L. 1389.
> Brampton occ. as preb. 12 Feb. 1379 (*Cal. MSS. D. & C. Wells* I 282). Langton occ. Feb. 1389 (*CPR. 1385–1389* p. 654). Brampton d. as preb. Sept. 1402/3 (*Cal. MSS. D. & C. Wells* II 39).

John Kyngman ?–1412.
> Res. this preb. before 24 Feb. 1412 (*Reg. Bubwith* I 113).

William Jakes 1412–1422.
> Coll. 24 Feb. 1412 (*Reg. Bubwith* I 113). Exch. preb. and ch. of Lymington, Hants, with Henry Penwortham for ch. of St Vedast, London, 14 Oct. 1422 (*ibid.* II 424).

Henry Penwortham 1422–1434.
> By exch. Oct. 1422. Preb. of Warminster al. Luxville 1434.

Richard Forest 1434–1435.
> Coll. 7 June 1434 (*Reg. Stafford (Bath and Wells)* II 163). D. before 29 Sept. 1435 (*ibid.* p. 186).

M. **John Burdett** 1435–?[1]
> Coll. 29 Sept. 1435 (*Reg. Stafford (Bath and Wells)* II 186).

William Bernham ?–1445/6.[1]
> D. as preb. Sept. 1445/6 (*Cal. MSS. D. & C. Wells* II 74).

M. **Richard Mayhew** B.Th. 1475–1504.
> Coll. 6 Sept. 1475 (*Reg. Stillington* p. 106). Bp. of Hereford 1504.

Baldwin de Lens ?–1508.
> Res. this preb. before 6 Feb. 1508 (*Reg. King* p. 126).

M. **Robert Asshcombe** M.A. 1508–?
> Coll. 6 Feb. 1508 (*Reg. King* p. 126). Adm. by proxy s.d. (*Cal. MSS. D. & C. Wells* II 207), adm. in person 1 Aug. 1509 (*ibid.* p. 214). Occ. 1515 (*Reg. King* p. 179). ? Held preb. until d. before 4 July 1528 (PCC 35 Porch).

William Stronge 1535.
> Occ. 1535 (*Valor* I 136).

---

[1] Bernham and Burdett appear to have exch. prebs. at some date, since Bernham was coll. to preb. of Combe Decima in 1426 and d. as preb. of Combe Sexta, 1445/6, and Burdett was coll. to preb. of Combe Sexta 1435 and d. as preb. of Combe Decima 1449, see p. 32.

PREBENDARIES OF COMBE SEPTIMA

Thomas de Donford ?–1352.
D. as preb. before 23 June 1352 (*CPP.* I 229).

Adam Trewelove 1352–?
Accepted prov. to preb. 23 June 1352 (*CPP.* I 229).

William de Odecumbe 1366.
Occ. Sept. 1366 (*Reg. Langham* p. 66). Occ. as can. of Wells 1377 (P.R.O., E 179/4/1).

M. Roger Page D.Cn.L. 1386.
Estate ratif. 20 July 1386 (*CPR. 1385–1389* p. 195).

John de Nottyngham ?–1389.
Exch. preb. with John Eyr for deanery of royal free chap., Hastings, Suss., 16 Oct. 1389 (*CPR. 1388–1392* p. 118).

John Eyr 1389–1391.
By exch. Oct. 1389. Adm. 2 Nov. (P.R.O., C 47/16/1 (19)). Exch. preb. with Thomas Ruggeley for ch. of Shoeburyness, Essex, 21 Apr. 1391 (Lond., Guildhall, Reg. Braybroke f. 85).

Thomas Ruggeley 1391–1392.
By exch. Apr. 1391. Exch. preb. with John Skyfteslyng for ch. of Swanscombe, Kent, 8 Apr. 1392 (Rochester, Reg. W. de Bottlesham ff. 25b–26).

M. John Skyfteslyng 1392–?
By exch. Apr. 1392.

John Brokhole ?–1434.
Exch. preb. with John Blodewell for ch. of Sturton-le-Steeple, Notts., 31 May 1434 (*Reg. Stafford (Bath and Wells)* II 163).

M. John Blodewell D.Cn.L. 1434–1437.
By exch. May 1434. Exch. preb. with Richard Hore for preb. of St Nicholas Penffoes, St Davids, 10 March 1437 (*Reg. Stafford (Bath and Wells)* II 203).

M. Richard Hore B.Cn. & C.L. 1437–1441.
By exch. March 1437. Preb. of Combe Duodecima and provost 1441.

M. John Arnald B.Th. 1441–1449.
Coll. 7 Dec. 1441 (*Reg. Stafford (Bath and Wells)* II 273). Res. before 27 Dec. 1449 (*Reg. Bekynton* I 133).

Robert Smyth 1449–?
Coll. 27 Dec. 1449 (*Reg. Bekynton* I 133).

M. Hugh Sugar *or* **Norris** D.C.L. 1460–1464.
Coll. 1 May 1460 (*Reg. Bekynton* I 344). Preb. of Litton 1464.

M. John Flemmyng M.A. 1464–1468.
Coll. 3 Oct. 1464 (*Reg. Bekynton* I 421). D. by 2 Jan. 1468 (*Reg. Stillington* p. 13).

M. John Mulcastre D.Th. ?–1472.
D. as preb. before 7 Jan. 1472 (*Reg. Stillington* p. 90).

John Lascy 1472–1479.
Coll. 7 Jan. 1472 (*Reg. Stillington* p. 90). Preb. of Whitelackington 1479.

M. Thomas Morton M.A. 1479–?
Coll. 22 May 1479 (*Reg. Stillington* p. 113). Possibly held preb. until year of death, 1496 (Ely, Reg. Alcock f. 110).

Thomas Parham 1496–?
Adm. 4 May 1496 (*Cal. MSS. D. & C. Wells* II 144). Occ. 1535 (*Valor* I 137).

PREBENDARIES OF COMBE OCTAVA

Walter de Pederton ?–1316.
D. as preb. before 24 Oct. 1316 (Reg. Drokensford ff. 99, 101b).

Thomas de Retford 1317–?
Coll. 7 Jan. 1317 (Reg. Drokensford f. 101b). Occ. 15 July 1329 (*Cal. MSS. D. & C. Wells* I 217).

William Banastre *junior* ?–1362.
Res. this preb. before 24 Apr. 1362 (*Reg. R. de Salopia* II 763).

John Warini de Wellesleigh 1362–1367.
Coll. 24 Apr. 1362 (*Reg. R. de Salopia* II 763). Exch. preb. with William Banastre for preb. of Easton in Gordano, 12 July 1367 (*CPR. 1364–1367* p. 423).

William Banastre *junior* (again) 1367–?
By exch. July 1367.

Thomas Banastre 1369–?
Royal gr. 29 Apr. 1369 (*CPR. 1367–1370* p. 245).

M. John Fraunceys B.Cn.L. ?–1413.
D. as preb. before 27 Jan. 1413 (*Reg. Bubwith* I 139).

Robert Appulton 1413–1418/19.
Coll. 27 Jan. 1413 (*Reg. Bubwith* I 139). D. Sept. 1418/19 (*Cal. MSS. D. & C. Wells* II 58).

M. Lewis Rede B.C.L. ?–1462.
Occ. 26 Apr. 1432 (*CPL.* VIII 441). D. before 4 Nov. 1462 (*Reg. Bekynton* I 377).

Walter Osborn 1462–?
Coll. 4 Nov. 1462 (*Reg. Bekynton* I 377).

M. John Taylour D.Th. ?–1493.
D. as preb. before 12 Apr. 1493 (*Reg. Stillington* p. 180).

M. John Retford B.Th. 1493–1503.
Coll. 12 Apr. 1493 (*Reg. Stillington* p. 180). Adm. 30 Apr. (*Cal. MSS. D. & C. Wells* II 128). D. before 20 Nov. 1503 (*CPR. 1494–1509* p. 343).

M. John Coale M.A. 1503–1536.
Royal gr. 20 Nov. 1503 (*CPR. 1494–1509* p. 343). Adm. by proxy 26 Nov. (*Cal. MSS. D. & C. Wells* II 174), in person 14 July 1509 (*ibid.* p. 214). Occ. 1535 (*Valor* I 136). D. by March 1536 (*Emden, Reg. Ox.* I 461).

M. Adam Howes ?–1541.
Res. this preb. before 18 June 1541 (*Reg. Bps., 1518–1559* p. 90).

M. Martin Tyndall 1541–?
Coll. 18 June 1541 (*Reg. Bps., 1518–1559* p. 90). ? Depriv. before 25 Nov. 1556, preb. then vac. because last incumbent had been depriv. (*ibid.* pp. 146–7).

PREBENDARIES OF COMBE NONA

William de Clopcote ?–1332.
Occ. as can. of Wells 26 Feb. 1326 (*Cal. MSS. D. & C. Wells* I 216). Exch. this preb. and ch. of Shepton Mallet, Som. with John de Sobbury for ch. of Cold Ashton, Glos., 30 Apr. 1332 (*Reg. R. de Salopia* I 93).

John de Sobbury 1332–?
By exch. Apr. 1332.

M. Richard Drayton B.Cn.L. 1379, 1391.
Prov. by pope Gregory XI, i.e. before 28 March 1378 (*CPL.* IV 365). Occ. as preb. 4 March 1379 (*Cal. MSS. D. & C. Wells* I 284). Estate ratif. 6 June 1391 (*CPR. 1388–1392* p. 420). Occ. as preb. of Whitelackington 1414.

Thomas Maddynglee ?–1417.
D. as preb. before 9 July 1417 (*Reg. Bubwith* I 281).

M. John Storthwayt B.C.L. 1417–1420.
Coll. 9 July 1417 (*Reg. Bubwith* I 281). Preb. of Easton in Gordano 1420.

M. Nicholas Burton 1420–1439/40.
Coll. 12 July 1420 (*Reg. Bubwith* II 392). D. Sept. 1439/Apr. 1440 (*Cal. MSS. D. & C. Wells* II 71; *Reg. Stafford (Bath and Wells)* II 249).

M. John Arnald B.Th. 1440–1441.
Coll. 28 Apr. 1440 (*Reg. Stafford (Bath and Wells)* II 249). Preb. of Combe Septima 1441.

M. William Skelton D.Cn. & C.L. 1441–1448.
Coll. 23 Nov. 1441 (*Reg. Stafford (Bath and Wells)* II 273). D. before 6 Apr. 1448 (*Reg. Bekynton* I 90).

Peter Courtenay 1448–1474.
Coll. 6 Apr. 1448 (*Reg. Bekynton* I 90). Res. before 24 Nov. 1474 (*Reg. Stillington* p. 103).

M. Philip Devenolde B.C.L. 1474–1493.
Coll. 24 Nov. 1474 (*Reg. Stillington* p. 103). D. before 2 Sept. 1493 (*ibid.* p. 186).

M. William Silk D.C.L. 1493–1508.
Coll. 2 Sept. 1493 (*Reg. Stillington* p. 186). Adm. 15 Sept. (*Cal. MSS. D. & C. Wells* II 103). D. before 11 July 1508 (*ibid.* pp. 208, 216).

M. Reginald West 1508–1509.
Adm. 11 July 1508 by proxy (*Cal. MSS. D. & C. Wells* II 208), in person 25 July (*ibid.*). Preb. of Holcombe 1509.

M. Robert Young M.A. 1509–?
Adm. 27 Feb. 1509 (*Cal. MSS. D. & C. Wells* II 212). ? Held preb until d. 31 Oct./ 7 Nov. 1515 (PCC 12 Holder).

Helesius Bodley 1535.
Occ. 1535 (*Valor* I 136).

PREBENDARIES OF COMBE DECIMA

Thomas de Haselschawe ?–1305.
Res. this preb. before 2 Oct. 1305 (*Cal. MSS. D. & C. Wells* I 191).

Hugh de Pencriz 1305–1320.
Adm. 2 Oct. 1305 (*Cal. MSS. D. & C. Wells* I 191). D. before 28 Dec. 1320 (Reg. Drokensford f. 159b).

M. Thomas de Aylington D.Th. 1321–1324.
Coll. 11 Jan. 1321 (Reg. Drokensford f. 160). Vac. preb. before 5 Dec. 1324 (*ibid.* f. 223).

William de Ayremynne 1324–1325.
Coll. 5 Sept. 1324 (Reg. Drokensford f. 223). Bp. of Norwich 1325.

Arnald de Malo Ingenio ?–1340.
Exch. preb. with Geoffrey de Chelcheheth for preb. of Cowpes, in Maldon, St Martin's-le-Grand colleg. ch., London, 28 May 1340 (*Reg. R. de Salopia* I 368).

Geoffrey de Chelcheheth 1340–?
By exch. May 1340.

Stephen Martin of Hull 1352.
Petitioned 10 June 1352 for papal conf. of coll. to preb. (*CPP.* I 228).

John de Ware 1366.
Occ. Sept. 1366 (*Reg. Langham* p. 65).

John Milward ?–1384.
John Blancherd 1379.
Milward occ. 12 Feb. 1379 (*Cal. MSS. D. & C. Wells* I 282). Blancherd occ. 22 Feb. (*ibid.* p. 283). Milward exch. preb. with Robert Clyst for ch. of Cold Ashton, Glos., 7 Apr. 1384 (Worcester, Reg. Wakefield f. 38b).

Robert Clyst 1384–?
By exch. Apr. 1384.

John Wareyn 1390.
Estate ratif. 23 May 1390 (*CPR. 1388–1392* p. 249).

William Derby 1419–1426.
Coll. 18 Oct. 1419 (*Reg. Bubwith* II 375). Res. before 10 Nov. 1426 (*Reg. Stafford (Bath and Wells)* I 42).

William Bernham 1426–?[1]
Coll. 10 Nov. 1426 (*Reg. Stafford (Bath and Wells)* I 42).

M. John Burdett ?–1449.[1]
D. as preb. before 7 Feb. 1449 (*Reg. Bekynton* I 109).

M. Thomas Gascoigne D.Th. 1449–?
Coll. 7 Feb. 1449 (*Reg. Bekynton* I 109). ? Held preb. until d. 12/22 March 1458 (*Eng. Hist. Rev.* liii 624).

M. Thomas Chaundeler D.Th. 1458–1463.
Coll. 15 March 1458 (*Reg. Bekynton* I 300). Preb. of Whitchurch 1463.

M. William King B.A. 1463–?
Coll. 31 Dec. 1463 (*Reg. Bekynton* I 407).

M. Thomas Tomyow D.Cn. & C.L. 1497–1518.
Adm. 1 June 1497 (*Cal. MSS. D. & C. Wells* II 147). D. before 12 Aug. 1518 (PCC 9 Ayloffe).

---

[1] Burdett and Bernham appear to have exch. prebs. at some date, see p. 28.

John Pennaude D.Cn.L. ?–1529/30.
D. as preb. Sept. 1529/30 (*Cal. MSS. D. & C. Wells* II 243).

Edmund Nowell 1535.
Occ. 1535 (*Valor* I 136).

PREBENDARIES OF COMBE UNDECIMA

M. John de Offord D.C.L. ?–1347.
Occ. 26 June 1346 (*CPR. 1345–1348* p. 129). Exch. preb. with John de Derby for preb. of Wiveliscombe, 21 Feb. 1347 (*Reg. R. de Salopia* II 540).

M. John de Derby 1347–1355.
By exch. Feb. 1347. Exch. preb. for the archdcnry of Barnstaple,[1] 1355 (Exeter, Reg. Grandisson III f. 105).

Thomas de Brantyngham 1367–1370.
Royal gr. 16 Oct. 1367 (*CPR. 1367–1370* p. 13). Bp. of Exeter 1370.

M. John Trevaur B.C.L. ?–1392.
Estate ratif. 14 Aug. 1386 (*CPR. 1385–1389* p. 208). Exch. preb. and precentorship with John Mere for ch. of Meifod, Montgom., 18 July 1392 (*CPR. 1391–1396* p. 122).

John Mere 1392–?
By exch. July 1392. Estate ratif. 8 Apr. 1393 (*CPR. 1391–1396* p. 245).

John Burnett ?–1409.
D. as preb. before 22 July 1409 (*Reg. Bubwith* I 60).

John Knyght 1409–1417.
Coll. 22 July 1409 (*Reg. Bubwith* I 60). Preb. of Buckland Dinham 1417.

John Osbern 1418–1419.
Coll. 7 Jan. 1418 (*Reg. Bubwith* I 297). Res. before 3 Oct. 1419 (*ibid.* II 375).

M. Henry Abendon D.Th. 1419–1438.
Coll. 3 Oct. 1419 (*Reg. Bubwith* II 375). D. before 10 March 1438 (*Reg. Stafford (Bath and Wells)* II 214).

M. John Stephens Lic.C.L. 1438–1467.
Coll. 10 March 1438 (*Reg. Stafford (Bath and Wells)* II 214). D. Nov. 1467 (*Emden, Reg. Ox.* III 1714).

Thomas Cowton ?–1488.
D. as preb. before 27 Feb. 1488 (*Cal. MSS. D. & C. Wells* II 110).

M. Oliver King D.Cn. & C.L. 1488–1490.
Adm. 27 Feb. 1488 (*Cal. MSS. D. & C. Wells* II 110). Archdcn. of Taunton 1490.

William Smythe 1490–?
Adm. 9 Aug. 1490 (*Cal. MSS. D. & C. Wells* II 119).

M. Richard Gardener 1505–1507.
Adm. 18 March 1505 (*Cal. MSS. D. & C. Wells* II 181). Res. before 7 Feb. 1507 (*ibid.* p. 200).

Roderic Diaz 1507–?
Adm. 7 Feb. 1507 (*Cal. MSS. D. & C. Wells* II 200).

[1] The name of the archdcn. of Barnstaple is not given. Hugh de Monyngton, according to Le Neve-Hardy, was then archdcn. He occ. as a can. of Wells in 1360 and 1365 (*Cal. MSS. D. & C. Wells* I 262, 268), but does not occur as preb. of Combe Undecima.

D

Richard Trobelfyld 1535.

Occ. 1535 (*Valor* I 136). ?Depriv. before 25 Nov. 1556; preb. then vac. because last incumbent had been depriv. (*Reg. Bps., 1518–1559* p. 147).

PREBENDARIES OF COMBE DUODECIMA[1]

M. William Brunell ?–1304.

Occ. 20 Nov. 1289 (*CPL.* I 506). D. before 6 Nov. 1304 (York, Reg. Sede Vac. f. 36b; *CPR. 1301–1307* p. 310).

Robert de Haselscawe ?–1330.

John de Sandale 1310–?

Haselscawe occ. 7 Aug. 1310 (Reg. Drokensford f. 52). Royal gr. to Sandale 11 Sept. (*CPR. 1307–1313* p. 277). Royal prohibn. 25 Oct. against persons disturbing Sandale's peaceful possession of preb. (*ibid.* p. 285). Haselscawe retained possession, occ. as preb. July 1311 (*Reg. Drokensford* p. 76). D. 27 March 1330 (Exeter, Reg. Grandisson III f. 14).

M. Peter de Berkeley 1330–1340.

Robert de Taunton 1333.

M. Alan de Cosneburg D.C.L. ?–1340.

M. John de Sancto Paulo 1340–1349.

Royal gr. to Berkeley 29 March 1330 (*CPR. 1327–1330* p. 503). Prohibn. 17 Apr. against all ecclesiastical persons acting in prejudice of k's right to pres. to preb. (*ibid.* p. 507). Taunton occ. as preb. 29 July 1333 (*CPL.* II 387). He appears to have been coll. by bp. since stated in royal writ that suit pending between bp. Salopia and Berkeley (*CPR. 1327–1330* p. 507). Cosneburg claimed preb. by virtue of prov. but unable to obtain possession, appealed to bp. of Exeter 9 May 1335 since preb. occupied by Taunton (Exeter, Reg. Grandisson II f. 188b). Preb. sequestrated 29 May 1336 (*ibid.* f. 199b). Sentence relaxed 16 Nov. and Cosneburg stated to be lawful claimant (*ibid.* f. 204b). Royal gr. to Berkeley revoked 1 Oct. 1340 (*CPR. 1340–1343* p. 65). Estate of de Sancto Paulo ratif. as preb. s.d. (*ibid.*). Cosneburg still claiming preb. but exch. Combe Duodecima and ch. of Sutton Courtenay, Berks., with de Sancto Paulo for preb. of Ryton, Lichfield, 23 Oct. (*Reg. R. de Salopia* I 373). Royal lic. for de Sancto Paulo to unite preb. with provostship, 3 July 1344 (*CPR. 1343–1345* p. 327). Abp. of Dublin 1349.

M. Andrew de Offord D.C.L. 1349–1359.

Prov. 10 Oct. 1349 (*CPP.* I 178). D. before 3 Feb. 1359 (*ibid.* p. 311).

Adam de Hilton 1359–?

Prov. 3 Feb. 1359 (*CPP.* I 311). Occ. 13 Oct. 1361 (*Cal. MSS. D. & C. Wells* I 264).

John de Newenham 1367–?

Royal gr. 12 Nov. 1367 (*CPR. 1367–1370* p. 40).

Roger de Holme 1370–?

Royal gr. 22 Apr. 1370 and 27 June (*CPR. 1367–1370* pp. 392, 442). Estate ratif. 22 Apr. (*ibid.* p. 390). Occ. 12 Feb. 1379 (*Cal. MSS. D. & C. Wells* I 282).

John Macclesfield 1389–1422.

[1] The preb. of Combe Duodecima was united to the provostship in 1344. The earlier provosts had claimed that the preb. of Wiveliscombe was attached to the provostship (*Cal. MSS. D. & C. Wells* I 250).

Walter Frelandi ?–1390.

Pileus de Prata Card. bp. of Tusculum. 1390–1394.
Royal gr. to Macclesfield 7 Dec. 1389 (*CPR. 1388–1392* p. 166). Frelandi called preb. and provost at d. before 29 Sept. 1390 (*CPL.* IV 385). De Prata prov. s.d. (*ibid.*). Res. before 19 May 1394 when title of Macclesfield as preb. and provost recognised (*ibid.* p. 473). Res. before 20 Feb. 1422 (*Reg. Bubwith* II 414).

William Skelton 1422–1441.
Coll. 20 Feb. 1422 (*Reg. Bubwith* II 414). Preb. of Combe Nona 1441.

M. Richard Hore B.Cn. & C.L. 1441–1449/50.
Coll. 30 Nov. 1441 (*Reg. Stafford (Bath and Wells)* II 273). D. 22 Nov. 1449/21 Jan. 1450 (*Som. Med. Wills 1501–1530* pp. 353–4).

John Trevenaunt 1450–1458.
Coll. 13 Apr. 1450 (*Reg. Bekynton* I 144). D. before 9 March 1458 (*ibid.* pp. 299–300).

John Garnesey 1458–1459.
Coll. 9 March 1458 (*Reg. Bekynton* I 299–300). D. before 21 June 1459 (*ibid.* p. 322).

M. Richard Swan M.A. 1459–1487.
Coll. 21 June 1459 (*Reg. Bekynton* I 322). D. before 30 Jan. 1487 (PCC I Milles; *Reg. Stillington* p. 142).

M. Richard Worthington B.Cn.L. 1487.
Coll. 11 Apr. 1487 (*Reg. Stillington* p. 142). Instal. by Hugh Sugar, treasurer, 24 Apr. (*Cal. MSS. D. & C. Wells* II 103–4). Instal. by d. and c. 6 June (*ibid.* p. 105). D. 24/27 Aug. (PCC 5 Milles; *Reg. Stillington* p. 149).

M. William Smythe B.C.L. 1487–1493.
Adm. by proxy 18 Sept. 1487 (*Cal. MSS. D. & C. Wells* II 106), in person 21 May 1488 (*ibid.* p. 111). Vac. preb. before 31 March 1493 (*Reg. Stillington* p. 190).[1]

M. Thomas Barowe D.C.L. 1493–?
Coll. 31 March 1493 (*Reg. Stillington* p. 190). Adm. 18 Apr. (*ibid.*). Possibly held preb. until d. 23 June/10 July 1499 (PCC 37 Horne).

M. John Barough 1499.
D. as preb. before 13 July 1499 (*Reg. King* p. 36).

M. Thomas Beaumont D.Cn. & C.L. 1499–1501.
Mand. adm. 13 July 1499 (*Reg. King* p. 36). Adm. 20 July (*Cal. MSS. D. & C. Wells* II 156). Preb. of Haselbere 1501.

John Becham 1501–?
Adm. 24 May 1501 (*Cal. MSS. D. & C. Wells* II 161). Occ. 1535 (*Valor* I 136).

PREBENDARIES OF COMBE TERCIADECIMA

John Beneyt 1361, 1366.
Occ. 10 Sept. 1361 (*Cal. MSS. D. & C. Wells* I 264) and 14 Sept. 1366 (*Reg. Langham* p. 17).

---

[1] William Smythe can probably be identified with William Smythe bp. of Coventry & Lichfield 1493–1495, since he vac. the preb. 1493, but this identification cannot be proved.

Edward Seylo 1379, 1386.

Occ. as can. of Wells 1377 (P.R.O., E. 179/4/1). Occ. as preb. of Combe Tercia-decima 22 Feb. 1379 (*Cal. MSS. D. & C. Wells* I 283) and 26 Apr. 1386 (*ibid.* p. 297).

Benedict atte Chirche ?–1408.

Res. this preb. 5 Apr. 1408 (*Reg. Bubwith* I 27).

M. **Eudo de la Zouche** D.C.L. 1408–?

Coll. 5 Apr. 1408 (*Reg. Bubwith* I 27). ? Until d. before 13 March 1414 (Norwich, Reg. Courtenay f. 78b).

M. **John Shirford** B.C.L. 1414–1417/18.

Coll. 15 March 1414 (*Reg. Bubwith* I 169). D. 1 Aug. 1417/25 Oct. 1418 (PCC 46 Marche).

John Godeford ?–1433.

Res. this preb. before 28 Jan. 1433 (*Reg. Stafford* (*Bath and Wells*) I 137).

M. **Thomas Bourgchier** M.A. 1433–1435.

Coll. 28 Jan. 1433 (*Reg. Stafford* (*Bath and Wells*) I 137). Bp. of Worcester 1435.

M. **John River** B.C.L. 1435.

M. **Richard Petteworth** B.Cn. & C.L. 1435–1457.

River prov. 12 March 1435 (*CPL.* VIII 236). Does not appear to have gained possession because Petteworth coll. 8 May (*Reg. Stafford* (*Bath and Wells*) II 183). Res. before 19 Dec. 1457 (*Reg. Bekynton* I 296).

M. **John Pakenham** B.Cn. & C.L. 1457–1460.

Coll. 19 Dec. 1457 (*Reg. Bekynton* I 296). Res. before 9 June 1460 (*ibid.* p. 346).

M. **Nicholas Kene** B.Cn. & C.L. 1460–?

Coll. 9 June 1460 (*Reg. Bekynton* I 346).

M. **William Preston** Sch.Th. 1473–1488/9.

Coll. 1 Aug. 1473 (*Reg. Stillington* p. 100). D. 30 Sept. 1488/25 June 1489 (PCC 35 Milles).

John Pryston ?–1490/1.[1]

D. as preb. Sept. 1490/1 (*Cal. MSS. D. & C. Wells* II 214).

M. **Robert Crofte** *or* **Froste** 1490–1494.

Adm. 3 July 1490 (*Cal. MSS. D. & C. Wells* II 119).[1] Res. before 15 Sept. 1494 (*Reg. Stillington* p. 195).

M. **John Arundell** B.Th. 1494–1496.

Coll. 15 Sept. 1494 (*Reg. Stillington* p. 195). Adm. 21 Sept. (*Cal. MSS. D. & C. Wells* II 137). Bp. of Coventry and Lichfield 1496.

M. **Thomas Jane** D.Cn.L. 1496–1499.

Adm. 29 Nov. 1496 (*Cal. MSS. D. & C. Wells* II 146). Bp. of Norwich 1499.

M. **George Sidenham** B.Cn. & C.L. 1499–?

Adm. 26 Oct. 1499 (*Cal. MSS. D. & C. Wells* II 156). ? Held preb. until d. before 21 Feb. 1524 (Salis., Reg. Audley f. 96b).

Christopher Sydenham ?–1524/5.

D. as preb. Sept. 1524/5 (*Cal. MSS. D. & C. Wells* II 241).

---

[1] Pryston and Crofte do not appear to have been rival claimants to this preb. Pryston's d. as preb. occ. only in the Michaelmas accounts of the dean and chapter of Wells, where the payments may be those made in the year after the death of the preb. See p. 19, n. 1.

M. **Reginald Baynbridge** B.Th. ?–1554/5.
Occ. 1535 (*Valor* I 136). D. 3 Nov. 1554/2 July 1555 (PCC 29 More; *Reg. Bps.*, *1518–1559* p. 139).

PREBENDARIES OF COMBE QUARTADECIMA

William de la Forde de Yatton ?–1324.
D. as preb. before 22 Jan. 1324 (Reg. Drokensford f. 217).

John de Wamberg 1324–?
Coll. 22 Jan. 1324 (Reg. Drokensford f. 217).

John Cok ?–1358.
D. as preb. before 24 May 1358 (*CPP.* I 308).

Poncius de Verreriis 1358–1361.
Prov. 24 May 1358 (*CPP.* I 308). D. before 23 Aug. 1361 (*Cal. MSS. D. & C. Wells* I 263).

Walter de Alderbury 1361–?
Mand. adm. 23 Aug. 1361 (*Cal. MSS. D. & C. Wells* I 263).

John de Neuport ?–1368.
Occ. June 1366 (*Reg. Sudbury* II 156). Exch. preb. with Thomas Strete de Knesworth for preb. of Shalford, 23 Nov. 1368 (*CPR. 1367–1370* p. 171).

Thomas Strete de Knesworth 1368–?
By exch. Nov. 1368. Occ. 12 Feb. 1379 (*Cal. MSS. D. & C. Wells* I 283).

M. **John Silvestre** *or* **Codeford** D.C.L. 1379–1381/2.
Adm. 9 July 1379 (*Cal. MSS. D. & C. Wells* I 258). D. Sept. 1381/2 (*ibid.* II 17).

John Yarnemothe ?–1397/8.
D. as preb. Sept. 1397/8 (*Cal. MSS. D. & C. Wells* II 31).

Robert Noel ?–1408.
Res. this preb. before 15 Feb. 1408 (*Reg. Giffard and Bowet* p. 73).

Thomas Cryshale 1408–1412.
Coll. 15 Feb. 1408 (*Reg. Giffard and Bowet* p. 73). Adm. 25 Feb. (*ibid.* p. 74). Exch. preb. with William Haukesworth for ch. of Shimpling, Norf., 4 Oct. 1412 (*Reg. Bubwith* I 129–30).

William Haukesworth 1412–?
By exch. Oct. 1412.

John Forest 1425.
Royal gr. 1 March 1425 (*CPR. 1422–1429* p. 270). Dean in Aug.

Nicholas Dixon 1425–1433.
Coll. 19 Sept. 1425 (*Reg. Stafford (Bath and Wells)* I 33). Res. before 1 July 1433 (*ibid.* p. 144).

M. **John Lukk** D.Th. 1433–1435.
Coll. 1 July 1433 (*Reg. Stafford (Bath and Wells)* I 144). D. before 10 Aug. 1435 (*ibid.* II 185).

William Stephens 1435–?
Coll. 10 Aug. 1435 (*Reg. Stafford (Bath and Wells)* II 185). Precentor 1440, or possibly res. 1438 when preb. of St Decumans.

M. Gilbert Kymer D.M., B.C.L. 1441–1463.
Coll. 28 May 1441 (*Reg. Stafford (Bath and Wells)* II 271). D. before 25 May 1463 (*Reg. Bekynton* I 386).

M. Robert Hunt *or* **Hurst** B.Cn. & C.L. 1463–1465.
Coll. 25 May 1463 (*Reg. Bekynton* I 386). D. before 1 Sept. 1465 (*Reg. Stillington* p. xxvi).

John Howeren 1465–?
Adm. 1 Sept. 1465 (*Reg. Stillington* p. xxvi).

M. Thomas Winterborne D.C.L. ?–1478.
D. as preb. before 7 Dec. 1478 (*Reg. Stillington* p. 112).

M. John de Gigliis D.Cn. & C.L. 1478–1497.
Coll. 7 Dec. 1478 (*Reg. Stillington* p. 112). Adm. 2 March 1487 (*Cal. MSS. D. & C. Wells* II 102). Bp. of Worcester 1497.

M. Henry Rawlyns B.C.L. 1497–?
Coll. 10 Dec. 1497 (Reg. King f. 11). Adm. 22 Dec. (*Cal. MSS. D. & C. Wells* II 149). ? Held preb. until d. 10 Sept. 1526/2 March 1527 (PCC 28 Porch).

Richard Pygott 1535, 1545.
Occ. 1535 (*Valor* I 135). Occ. as preb. of Wells Nov. 1545 (*L. & P.* xx ii No. 909 (53)).

PREBENDARIES OF COMBE QUINTADECIMA

William de Weston ?–1340.
Exch. preb. with Nicholas de Ilford for chap. of Claverham, Som., 26 May 1340 (*Reg. R. de Salopia* I 368).

Nicholas de Ilford 1340–?
By exch. May 1340.

M. John Welborne D.C.L. 1379, 1390.
Occ. 12 Feb. 1379 (*Cal. MSS. D. & C. Wells* I 282). Estate ratif. 6 March 1390 (*CPR. 1388–1392* p. 226).

M. Robert Wytton D.C.L. 1401.
Estate ratif. 13 May 1401 (*CPR. 1399–1401* p. 482).

Robert Parfit 1438–1439.
Coll. 13 March 1438 (*Reg. Stafford (Bath and Wells)* II 214). Res. before 27 Apr. 1439 (*ibid.* p. 236).

M. Nicholas Carent B.C.L. 1439–1446.
Coll. 27 Apr. 1439 (*Reg. Stafford (Bath and Wells)* II 236). Dean 1446.

M. John Morton D.Th. 1446–1447.
Coll. 28 Aug. 1446 (*Reg. Bekynton* I 67). Preb. of Whitchurch 1447.

M. Thomas Bromehale B.Cn. & C.L. 1447–1463.
Coll. 25 July 1447 (*Reg. Bekynton* I 79). Preb. of Whitelackington 1463.

M. Robert Purviour B.A. 1463–?
Coll. 3 Jan. 1463 (*Reg. Bekynton* I 380). Occ. 26 March (*ibid.* II 541).

Henry Edyall ?–1487.
Res. this preb. before 17 Oct. 1487 when preb. of St Decumans (*Cal. MSS. D. & C. Wells* II 108).

M. John Vowell D.C.L. 1487–1502.
Adm. 17 Oct. 1487 (*Cal. MSS. D. & C. Wells* II 108). D. 29 Sept./6 Oct. 1502 (*ibid*. pp. 172, 168).

William Hichman O.Cist. Abbot of Stratford. 1502–1506.
Adm. 6 Oct. 1502 (*Cal. MSS. D. & C. Wells* II 168). Res. before 3 Aug. 1506 (*ibid*. p. 195).

John Thomson 1506–?
Adm. 3 Aug. 1506 (*Cal. MSS. D. & C. Wells* II 195).

Anthony Barbour 1535.
Occ. 1535 (*Valor* I 136).

PREBENDARIES OF COMPTON BISHOP

Ingelard de Warle 1308–1317.
Royal gr. 15 Dec. 1308 (*CPR. 1307/1313* p. 98). D. before 24 Oct. 1317 (*CPR. 1317–1321* p. 37).

M. Gilbert de Bruer ?–1349.
Exch. preb. with John de Carleton for preb. of Haselbere, c. 29 Apr. 1349 (*CPP.* I 157).

M. John de Carleton D.C.L. 1349–?
By exch. Apr. 1349. ? Held preb. until d. before 27 Aug. 1361 (*Cal. MSS. D. & C. Wells* I 263).

John de Horsington 1366.
Occ. Sept. 1366 (*Reg. Langham* p. 66). ? Held preb. until d. Sept. 1381/2 (*Cal. MSS. D. & C. Wells* II 17).

John Menhir 1386.
Royal gr. 17 Sept. 1386 (*CPR. 1385–1389* p. 212).

Thomas Somerset 1386.
Estate ratif. 20 Nov. 1386 (*CPR. 1385–1389* p. 239).

Christopher Marini Card. pr. of S. Cyriacus. ?–1391.
Prov. after d. of Somerset at curia n.d. (*CPL.* IV 383, 384). Exch. preb. with William Waltham for preb. of Twiford, St Paul's, London, 4 Jan. 1391 (*ibid*.).

M. William Waltham 1391–1395.
By exch. Jan. 1391. Exch. preb. with John Coldseye for preb. of Chalke, Wilton conventual ch., Wilts., 20 Apr./21 June 1395 (Salis., Reg. Waltham f. 163; *CPL.* IV 505).

John Coldseye 1395–1401.
By exch. Apr./June 1395. D. before 6 Aug. 1401 (*CPR. 1399–1401* p. 527).

Richard Pittes 1401–?
Royal gr. 6 Aug. 1401 (*CPR. 1399–1401* p. 527).

Nicholas Carlton ?–1416.
Exch. preb. with Thomas Polton for archdcnry of Taunton, 1 Sept. 1416 (*Reg. Bubwith* I 243–4).

M. Thomas Polton B.Cn. & C.L. 1416–1417.
By exch. Sept. 1416. Exch. preb. with John Hody for ch. of Brightwell, Berks., 12 Nov. 1417 (*Reg. Bubwith* I 294).

M. **John Hody** B.C.L. 1417–1440.
By exch. Nov. 1417. D. before 19 March 1440 (*Reg. Stafford (Bath and Wells)* II 247).

Fulk Bermyngeham 1440–?
Coll. 19 March 1440 (*Reg. Stafford (Bath and Wells)* II 247). Occ. 1457/8 (*Cal. MSS. D. & C. Wells* II 89).

M. **John Alcock** D.C.L. ?–1465.
Res. this preb. 1 Sept. 1465 (*Reg. Stillington* p. xxvi).

M. **John Bourgchier** 1470.
Occ. 27 May 1470 (*Reg. Stillington* p. 35).

Peter Carmelian 1496–?
Adm. 7 March 1496 (*Cal. MSS. D. & C. Wells* II 143). Occ. 5 May 1511 (*Reg. King* p. 150).

M. **Edward Fox** D.Th. ?–1535.
Occ. 17 Feb. 1529 (*Reg. Bps., 1518–1559* p. 57). Occ. 1535 (*Valor* I 134). Bp. of Hereford in Aug.

The next preb. of Compton Bishop of whom there is record is James Bisse, instal. 12 Oct. 1598 (*Cal. MSS. D. & C. Wells* II 337).

PREBENDARIES OF COMPTON DUNDON

John de Sandale 1309–1310.
Royal gr. 16 May 1309 (*CPR. 1307–1313* p. 115). Preb. of Wiveliscombe and Combe Duodecima 1310.

William de Hanlo ?–1313.
Res. this preb. Feb. 1313 when preb. of Ilton (Reg. Drokensford f. 136).

Hervey de Staunton 1313–?
Coll. 13 March 1313 (Reg. Drokensford f. 136). Occ. 26 June 1327 (*Cal. MSS. D. & C. Wells* I 205–6).

Thomas de Drokensford 1327.
Coll. revoked 9 Nov. 1327 (*Reg. Drokensford* p. 275). Preb. of Ilton 1328.

Alan de Hothom 1328–?
Coll. Jan. 1328 (*Reg. Drokensford* p. 279). Occ. 1 Apr. 1344 (*Reg. R. de Salopia* II 515).

William Vigerous 1352.
Estate ratif. 12 March 1352 (*CPR. 1350–1354* pp. 240–1).

Thomas Madefrey 1366.
Occ. Sept. and Nov. 1366 (*Reg. Langham* pp. 66, 71).

M. **Roger Harewell** B.C.L. ?–1430.
Estate ratif. 4 July 1376 (*CPR. 1374–1377* p. 278). Royal gr. 15 Aug. 1386 (*CPR. 1385–1389* p. 207). Res. before 9 Jan. 1430 (*Reg. Stafford (Bath and Wells)* I 74–5).

Henry Blakmoor 1430–1440.
Coll. 9 Jan. 1430 (*Reg. Stafford (Bath and Wells)* I 74–5). D. before 12 May 1440 (*ibid.* II 251).

M. **Richard Leyott** D.C.L. 1440–1449.
  Coll. 12 May 1440 (*Reg. Stafford (Bath and Wells)* II 251). D. before 3 Feb. 1449 (*Reg. Bekynton* I 109).

  Stephen Morpath 1449–1469/70.
  Coll. 3 Feb. 1449 (*Reg. Bekynton* I 108–9). D. Sept. 1469/70 (*Cal. MSS. D. & C. Wells* II 92).

M. **Thomas Overary** B.C.L. ?–1493.
  Occ. 22 Sept. 1470 (*Reg. Stillington* p. 37). D. 18/28 July 1493 (PCC 4 Vox; *CPR. 1485–1494* p. 430).

  Thomas Colson 1493–1501.
  Coll. 10 Aug. 1493 (*Reg. Stillington* p. 185). Adm. 20 Aug. (*Cal. MSS. D. & C. Wells* II 130). Res. before 24 May 1501 (*ibid.* p. 161).

M. **Thomas Cornish** O.St. J. of Jer., M.A. Bp. of Tine. 1501–1513.
  Adm. 24 May 1501 (*Cal. MSS. D. & C. Wells* II 161). D. 31 March/20 July 1513 (PCC 18 Fetiplace).

M. **Thomas Wolsey** D.Th. 1513–1514.
  Adm. 30 Aug. 1513 (*Cal. MSS. D. & C. Wells* II 234). Bp. of Lincoln 1514.

  Andrew Ammonius ?–1518.
  Occ. 14 Aug. 1517 (*Reg. King* p. 187). D. before 30 Apr. 1518 (PCC 7 Ayloffe).

M. **Peter Vannes** B.Th. 1534, 1556.
  Occ. 20 May 1534 (*Reg. Bps., 1518–1559* p. 71). Occ. 28 Feb. 1556 (*ibid.* p. 140). ? Held preb. until d. before 3 May 1564 (Lond., Guildhall, Reg. Grindal f. 133).

PREBENDARIES OF CUDWORTH

M. **Peter de Dene** 1300–?
  Adm. 2 Jan. 1300 (*Cal. MSS. D. & C. Wells* I 159).

  Richard de Rodeneye ?–1345.
  Exch. preb. with Bartholomew Tirel for preb. of Litton, 13 Jan. 1345 (*Reg. R. de Salopia* II 522).

  Bartholomew Tirel 1345–?
  By exch. Jan. 1345. Occ. as preb. of Wells 8 May 1348 (*Reg. R. de Salopia* I 419).

M. **Richard de Carleton** 1366.
  Occ. as can. of Wells 15 Feb. 1348 (*CPL.* III 260). Occ. as preb. of Cudworth 18 Nov. 1366 (*Reg. Langham* p. 68). D. Sept. 1381/2 (*Cal. MSS. D. & C. Wells* II 10, 17).

  Thomas atte Ende ?–1393.
  Exch. preb. with Henry Harborough for ch. of Banham, Norf., 20 Dec. 1393 (Norwich, Reg. Despenser ff. 185–185b).

  Henry Harborough 1393–1417.
  By exch. Dec. 1393. Estate ratif. 7 Feb. 1394 (*CPR. 1391–1396* pp. 368, 377) and 31 Oct. 1399 (*CPR. 1399–1401* p. 27). Res. 17 June 1417 (*Reg. Bubwith* I 282).

  Humphrey Radeley 1417–1429.
  Coll. 24 July 1417 (*Reg. Bubwith* I 282). Exch. preb. with John Conge for preb. of Offley, Lichfield, 23 June 1429 (*Reg. Stafford (Bath and Wells)* I 70).

John Conge 1429–1451.
By exch. June 1429. D. before 13 June 1451 (*Reg. Bekynton* i 164).

John Haydour 1451–1452.
Coll. 13 June 1451 (*Reg. Bekynton* i 164). D. before 17 May 1452 (*ibid.* p. 185).

M. **William Fulford** B.Cn. & C.L. 1452–1475.
Coll. 17 May 1452 (*Reg. Bekynton* i 185). D. before 27 Oct. 1475 (*Reg. Stillington* p. 107).

M. **Edmund Audley** M.A. 1475–1480.
Coll. 27 Oct. 1475 (*Reg. Stillington* p. 107). Bp. of Rochester 1480.

M. **Thomas Rayns** M.A. ?–1494.
Exch. preb. with Thomas Cornish for ch. of St Jude, Axbridge, Som., 18 Oct. 1494 (*Reg. Stillington* p. 197).

M. **Thomas Cornish** O.St.J. of Jer., M.A. Bp. of Tine. 1494–1501.
By exch. Oct. 1494. Preb. of Compton Dundon 1501.

M. **Hugh Ynge** D.Th. 1501–1503.
Adm. 24 June 1501 (*Cal. MSS. D. & C. Wells* ii 162). Preb. of Eastharptree 1503.

M. **Thomas Goldwege** 1503–1513.
Royal gr. 18 Oct. 1503 (*CPR. 1494–1509* p. 334). Adm. 24 Oct. (*Cal. MSS. D. & C. Wells* ii 173). D. before 21 Nov. 1513 (*ibid.* p. 235).

M. **James Fitzjames** M.A. 1513–?
Adm. 21 Nov. 1513 (*Cal. MSS. D. & C. Wells* ii 235).

M. **James Gilbert** ?–1557.
Occ. 1535 (*Valor* i 135). D. before 1 Jan. 1557 (*Reg. Bps., 1518–1559* p. 147).

PREBENDARIES OF DINDER

M. **Richard de Plumstock** ?–1323.
Occ. 4 Nov. 1310 (*CPR. 1307–1313* p. 289). D. before 14 Dec. 1323 (Reg. Drokensford f. 201b).

M. **John de Brabazon** D.Th. 1323–?
Coll. 14 Dec. 1323 (Reg. Drokensford f. 201b). Occ. as can. of Wells 8 Jan. 1330 (*Reg. R. de Salopia* i 65).

M. **Alan de Hothom** 1331.
Estate ratif. 12 Oct. 1331 (*CPR. 1330–1334* p. 178).

William de Stowe 1333, 1351.
Occ. 30 July 1333 (*CPL.* ii 377). Estate ratif. 11 March 1351 (*CPR. 1350–1354* p. 52).

William Basset ?–1367.
Occ. 17 Oct. 1366 (*Reg. Sudbury* ii 175). Exch. preb. with Thomas de Aston for preb. in Norton colleg. ch., co. Dur., 22 Nov. 1367 (*CPR. 1367–1370* p. 33).

M. **Thomas de Aston** 1367–1382.
By exch. Nov. 1367. Exch. preb. with Adam Davenport for preb. Centum Solidorum, Lincoln, 17 March 1382 (Linc., Reg. x (Buckingham) f. 118).

M. **Adam Davenport** 1382–?
By exch. March 1382. Adm. 5 May (*Cal. MSS. D. & C. Wells* i 291).

M. Michael Sergeaux D.C.L. ?–1397.
M. Thomas Sparkeford B.C.L. 1388–1389.
    John Menhir 1389.
    William Excestre 1390–1392.
    Estate of Sergeaux ratif. 3 July 1388 (*CPR. 1385–1389* p. 480). Royal gr. to Sparke-
ford 1 Oct. (*ibid.* p. 509). Royal gr. to Menhir 5 July 1389 (*CPR. 1388–1392* p. 83).
Sparkeford had been gr. preb. of Eastharptree 3 July and probably then res. claim to
Dinder (*ibid.* p. 75). Royal gr. to Excestre 12 Apr. 1390 (*ibid.* p. 236). Probably res.
claim to Dinder 1392 when preb. of Combe Tercia, since Sergeaux called preb. of
Dinder at d., by 3 Sept. 1397 (Salis., Reg. Medford f. 51b; *Cal. MSS. D. & C. Wells*
II 32).

    Hugh de Hanworth 1397–1408.
    Estate ratif. 30 Sept. 1397 (*CPR. 1396–1399* p. 199) and 13 Nov. 1399 (*CPR.
1399–1401* p. 55). Res. before 21 Feb. 1408 (*Reg. Giffard and Bowet* p. 73).

    John Halywell 1408–1411.
    Coll. 21 Feb. 1408 (*Reg. Giffard and Bowet* p. 73). Estate ratif. 29 June (*CPR.
1405–1408* p. 370). Exch. preb. with Thomas Feryby for preb. of Fawkeners, in Good
Easter, St Martin's-le-Grand colleg. ch., London, 10 July 1411 (*Reg. Bubwith* I 106).

    Thomas Feryby 1411–1426.
    By exch. July 1411. Exch. preb. with Richard Banastre for St Radegund's free
chap., St Paul's, London, 18/22 Jan. 1426 (St Paul's MS. WD 13 f. 112b/109b; *Reg.
Stafford (Bath and Wells)* I 35).

    Richard Banastre 1426–1431.
    By exch. Jan. 1426. D. or res. by 6 Apr. 1431 (*Reg. Stafford (Bath and Wells)* I 97).
M. Nicholas Upton B.Cn. & C.L. 1431–1452.
    Coll. 6 Apr. 1431 (*Reg. Stafford (Bath and Wells)* I 97). Res. before 19 Jan. 1452
(*Reg. Bekynton* I 176).
M. Thomas Swyft B.Cn. & C.L. 1452–1453.
    Coll. 19 Jan. 1452 (*Reg. Bekynton* I 176). Res. before 3 Dec. 1453 (*ibid.* p. 222).
M. John Morton D.C.L. 1453–1476.
    Coll. 3 Dec. 1453 (*Reg. Bekynton* I 222). Preb. of St Decumans 1476.[1]
M. John Dudley 1476.
    Coll. 13 Feb. 1476 (*Reg. Stillington* p. 108). Res. or d. before 1 July (*ibid.*).
    John Lichefeld 1476–?
    Coll. 1 July 1476 (*Reg. Stillington* p. 108).

    William Pavy ?–1493.
    Res. this preb. before 12 Apr. 1493 (*Reg. Stillington* p. 180). Called Henry Pavy 22
Apr. (*Cal. MSS. D. & C. Wells* II 128).

    John Menyman 1493–1497.
    Coll. 12 Apr. 1493 (*Reg. Stillington* p. 180). Adm. 22 Apr. (*Cal. MSS. D. & C.
Wells* II 128). D. before 21 July 1497 (Reg. King f. 8b).
M. John Lugwardyn 1497–1499.
    Coll. 21 July 1497 (Reg. King f. 8b). Adm. 25 July (*Cal. MSS. D. & C. Wells* II
147). Preb. of Timberscombe 1499.

---

[1] The admittance of Thomas Overary to this preb. on 23 Dec. 1465 appears to have been an error
(*Reg. Stillington* p. xxviii). Morton held the preb. until 1476.

William Thirlow 1499–1501.

Coll. 15 Apr. 1499 (*Reg. King* p. 29). Adm. 9 June (*Cal. MSS. D. & C. Wells* II 156). Res. or d. before 15 June 1501 (*ibid.* p. 162).

M. John Streynsham 1501–1509.

Adm. 15 June 1501 (*Cal. MSS. D. & C. Wells* II 162). Res. before 30 Aug. 1509 (*ibid.* p. 215).

M. Robert Gumby *or* **Austeyne** 1509–?

Adm. 30 Aug. 1509 (*Cal. MSS. D. & C. Wells* II 215). Occ. 26 March 1510 (*ibid.* p. 220). Occ., not called preb., 5 Dec. 1528 (*Reg. Bps., 1518–1559* p. 50).

Robert Crocket 1535.

Occ. 1535 (*Valor* I 135).

PREBENDARIES OF DULTINGCOTE

Michael de Drokensford 1311–1361.

Coll. Apr. 1311 (*Reg. Drokensford* p. 40). Entry cancelled, coll. again 2 Oct. 1316 and 11 June 1321 (*ibid.* pp. 113, 203). D. before 11 Oct. 1361 (*Cal. MSS. D. & C. Wells* I 264–5).

John Power 1361–?
John Coddington 1362.

Power adm. 11 Oct. 1361 (*Cal. MSS. D. & C. Wells* I 264–5). Coddington claimed preb. by prov., bp. held enquiry 21 July 1362 concerning title of Power to preb. (*Reg. R. de Salopia* II 769–70). Coddington res. 22 July (*ibid.*). Power occ. 18 Nov. 1366 (*Reg. Langham* p. 68).

M. Robert Rygge D.Th. ?–1410.

Estate ratif. 21 Feb. and 12 Aug. 1386 (*CPR. 1385–1389* pp. 117, 208). D. before 16 Apr. 1410 (*Reg. Bubwith* I 78).

Thomas Shelford 1410–1419.

Coll. 16 Apr. 1410 (*Reg. Bubwith* I 78). Preb. of St Decumans 1419.

John Roland 1419–?

Coll. 3 May 1419 (*Reg. Bubwith* II 357). ? Held preb. until d. before 12 July 1426 (*Reg. Stafford (Bath and Wells)* I 40).

M. Peter Stukeley B.C.L. 1427–1437.

Coll. 5 Dec. 1427 (*Reg. Stafford (Bath and Wells)* I 58). Preb. of St Decumans 1437.

John Southwode 1437–1441.

Coll. 4 Feb. 1437 (*Reg. Stafford (Bath and Wells)* II 202). D. before 11 Apr. 1441 (*ibid.* p. 269).

M. Thomas Bekynton D.C.L. 1441–1443.

Coll. 11 Apr. 1441 (*Reg. Stafford (Bath and Wells)* II 269). Bp. of Bath and Wells 1443.

M. William Bykonill D.C.L. 1443–1448.

Coll. 4 May 1443 (*Reg. Stafford (Bath and Wells)* II 283). D. before 5 Nov. 1448 (*Reg. Bekynton* I 110).

M. Thomas Boleyn 1448–1472.

Coll. 5 Nov. 1448 (*Reg. Bekynton* I 110). D. before 19 Feb. 1472 (*Reg. Stillington* p. 91).

M. Henry Sharp D.C.L. 1472–1489.
Coll. 5 May 1472 (*Reg. Stillington* p. 91). D. 26 Apr. 1489 (Brit. Mus., Cotton MS. Faustina B. viii f. 3b).

William Brereton 1489–?
Coll. 25 May 1489 (*Reg. Stillington* p. 158). Adm. 9 June (*Cal. MSS. D. & C. Wells* II 115).

M. Robert Shorton D.Th. 1535.
Occ. 1535 (*Valor* I 133). D. 17 Oct. (Cambridge, Corpus Christi College, MS. 108 f. 90).

PREBENDARIES OF EASTHARPTREE

Louis de Beaumont ?–1317.
Held preb. before el. as bp. of Durham 1317. Preb. said 28 May 1318 to be vac. by res. (*Reg. Drokensford* p. 13).

Lawrence Weston
John de Sancto Paulo 1339–1340.
Richard de Thistleden ?–1348.
Royal gr. to de Sancto Paulo 3 Aug. 1339 (*CPR. 1338–1340* p. 391). Preb. of Combe Duodecima 1340. Thistleden occ. as preb. 28 Jan. (*Reg. R. de Salopia* I 427–8). Weston was said to have held preb. before Thistleden (*Cal. MSS. D. & C. Wells* I 161). Thistleden held preb. until d. 4 Nov. 1348 (*Reg. R. de Salopia* II 690).

M. Henry de Harewedon ?–1349.
Estate ratif. 12 Nov. 1348 (*CPR. 1348–1350* p. 205). Res. before 1 May 1349 (*Reg. R. de Salopia* II 593).

Henry de Ingleby 1349–?
Coll. 1 May 1349 (*Reg. R. de Salopia* II 593).

John Lumbard ?–1380/1.
Adam Dele 1368–?
Richard Spicer 1371, 1379.
Lumbard occ. as preb. 1362 (*Cal. MSS. D. & C. Wells* I 161) and Sept. 1366 (*Reg. Langham* p. 64). Royal gr. to Dele 16 Oct. 1368 (*CPR. 1367–1370* p. 153). Estate of Spicer ratif. 24 Nov. 1371 (*CPR. 1370–1374* p. 13), and occ. as preb. 12 Feb. 1379 (*Cal. MSS. D. & C. Wells* I 282). Lumbard called preb. at d. Sept. 1380/1 (*ibid.* II 16).

M. Thomas Sparkeford B.C.L. 1389–?
Royal gr. 3 July 1389 (*CPR. 1388–1392* p. 75). ? Held preb. until archdcn. of Taunton 1395.

Hugh Bulneye ?–1397/8.
D. as preb. Sept. 1397/8 (*Cal. MSS. D. & C. Wells* II 31).

M. Ralph Canon ?–1422.
Occ. 13 Dec. 1398 (*CPL.* v 257). D. 18 Apr./5 June 1422 (PCC 54 Marche; *Reg. Bubwith* II 419).

M. William Spaldyngton B.Cn.L. 1422–1445.
Coll. 5 June 1422 (*Reg. Bubwith* II 419). D. before 2 Aug. 1445 (*Reg. Bekynton* I 43).

M. Robert Stillington D.C.L. 1445–1446.
Coll. 2 Aug. 1445 (*Reg. Bekynton* I 43). Exch. preb. with Andrew Holes for preb. of Mathry, St Davids, 3 Feb. 1446 (*ibid.* p. 58).

M. **Andrew Holes** D.Cn.L. 1446.
By exch. Feb. 1446. Archdcn. of Taunton 13 Feb.

M. **William Hoper** D.C.L. 1446-1454.
Coll. 8 May 1446 (*Reg. Bekynton* I 62). D. before 19 May 1454 (*ibid.* p. 232).

M. **Hugh Pavy** 1454-1485.
Coll. 19 May 1454 (*Reg. Bekynton* I 232). Bp. of St Davids 1485.

M. **Thomas Harris** B.Cn.L. 1489-1503.
Adm. 19 Dec. 1489 (*Cal. MSS. D. & C. Wells* II 118). Preb. of Henstridge 1503.

M. **Hugh Ynge** D.Th. 1503-?
Coll. 24 Aug. 1503 (*Reg. King* p. 83). Adm. 29 Aug. (*Cal. MSS. D. & C. Wells* II 172). Occ. 1 July 1513 (*ibid.* p. 233). Abp. of Dublin 1521.[1]

M. **Richard Pates** ?-1542.
Occ. 1535 (*Valor* I 135). Exiled 1542 (*L. & P.* XVII No. 28 (40)).

PREBENDARIES OF EASTON IN GORDANO

M. **Anthony de Bradeneye** 1299-1325.
Adm. 2 June 1299 (*Cal. MSS. D. & C. Wells* I 159). D. before 2 Jan. 1325 (Reg. Drokensford f. 225).

M. **James de Berkeley** D.Th. ?-1326.
Res. this preb. when bp. of Exeter Dec. 1326 (*Reg. Drokensford* p. 266).

Eudo de Berkeley 1327-1328.
Coll. 4 Apr. 1327 (*Reg. Drokensford* p. 266). D. before 1 Sept. 1328 (*ibid.* p. 291).

M. **Peter de Berkeley** 1328-1331.
Coll. 1 Sept. 1328 (*Reg. Drokensford* p. 291). Exch. preb. with Walter de Brinton for preb. in Glasney colleg. ch., Cornw., 8 July 1331 (*Reg. R. de Salopia* I 67).

Walter de Brinton 1331-1337.
By exch. July 1331. Exch. preb. with William de Salton for ch. of Stanton St Bernard, Wilts., 3/13 July 1337 (Salis., Reg. Wyville II ii f. 50b; *Reg. R. de Salopia* I 306-7).

M. **William de Salton** 1337-1353.
By exch. July 1337. Exch. preb. with John de Sydenhale for preb. of Warminster al. Luxville, 4 Sept. 1353 (*Reg. R. de Salopia* II 724-5).

M. **John de Sydenhale** M.A. 1353-?
By exch. Sept. 1353.

William Banastre *junior* ?-1367.
Exch. preb. with John Warini de Wellesleigh for preb. of Combe Octava, 12 July 1367 (*CPR. 1364-1367* p. 423).

John Warini de Wellesleigh 1367-?
By exch. July 1367. Occ. as can. of Wells 1377 (P.R.O., E 179/4/1).

M. **Thomas Weston** Lic.C.L. 1389.
Estate ratif. 15 June 1389 (*CPR. 1388-1392* p. 48).

[1] Ynge's appointment as abp. of Dublin is not necessarily an indication that he res. his preb. at this date, 1521. He had been appointed bp. of Meath in 1512 and occ. as preb. of Eastharptree after that date, and William Rokeby, the previous abp. of Dublin, cons. 1512, had been coll. to the archdcnry of Surrey 27 March 1519 (Winchester, Reg. Fox IV ff. 2b, 14b).

M. **John Maundour** D.Th. ?–1400.
Estate ratif. 28 Sept. 1391 (*CPR. 1388–1392* p. 485). D. by 18 Feb. 1400 (*CPL.* v 340).

William Dolbera 1400–1420.
Prov. 18 Feb. 1400 (*CPL.* v 340). Estate ratif. 14 June (*CPR. 1399–1401* p. 307). D. before 25 Apr. 1420 (*Reg. Bubwith* II 388).

William Skelton 1420.
Coll. 25 Apr. 1420 (*Reg. Bubwith* II 388). Res. before 7 July (*ibid.* p. 392).

M. **John Storthwayt** B.C.L. 1420–1435.
Coll. 7 July 1420 (*Reg. Bubwith* II 392). Preb. of Litton 1435.

M. **Nicholas Billesden** D.C.L. 1435–1441.
Coll. 31 May 1435 (*Reg. Stafford (Bath and Wells)* II 183). D. before 27 May 1441 (*ibid.* p. 271).

Robert Parfit 1441–1455.
Coll. 27 May 1441 (*Reg. Stafford (Bath and Wells)* II 271). D. before 7 Nov. 1455 (*Reg. Bekynton* I 259).

M. **John Spekyngton** M.A. 1455–1463.
Coll. 7 Nov. 1455 (*Reg. Bekynton* I 259). D. before 1 Jan. 1463 (*ibid.* p. 380).

John Roche 1463–?
Coll. 1 Jan. 1463 (*Reg. Bekynton* I 380). Occ. 5 Aug. 1474 (*Reg. Stillington* p. 56).

M. **William Smythe** B.C.L. ?–1488.[1]
Res. this preb. before 20 March 1488 (*Cal. MSS. D. & C. Wells* II 110).

M. **John Seymour** 1488–?
Adm. 20 March 1488 (*Cal. MSS. D. & C. Wells* II 110). D. Sept. 1502/3 (*ibid.* p. 172).[2]

Thomas Hay ?–1501.
D. as preb. before 8 Nov. 1501[2] (*Reg. King* p. 62).

Henry Haywardine 1501–?
Coll. 8 Nov. 1501 (*Reg. King* p. 62).

M. **Christopher Urswick** D.Cn.L. 1502/3–1509.
Adm. 1502/3 (*Cal. MSS. D. & C. Wells* II 169). Res. before 14 Dec. 1509 (*ibid.* p. 219).

M. **Thomas Linacre** D.M. 1509–?
Adm. 14 Dec. 1509 (*Cal. MSS. D. & C. Wells* II 219).

M. **Richard Wyott** D.Th. 1522.
Occ. 15 July 1522 (*Reg. Bps., 1518–1559* p. 22).

M. **Maurice Brekynshall** 1525, 1535.
Occ. 24 March 1525 (*Reg. Bps., 1518–1559* p. 39). Occ. 1535 (*Valor* I 134).

---

[1] William Smythe had been coll. to the preb. of Combe Duodecima in 1487, but was not adm. in person until 21 May 1488 (*Cal. MSS. D. & C. Wells* II 106, 111).
[2] Seymour and Hay do not appear to have been rival claimants. Seymour's d. occurs in the Michaelmas accounts where the payment may have been that made to the escheator after the d. of a preb. See p. 19, n. 1.

PREBENDARIES OF HASELBERE

John de Berewyk ?–1312.
D. as preb. before 2 July 1312 (Reg. Drokensford f. 41).

M. **John de Bruton** 1312–1339.
Coll. 2 July 1312 (Reg. Drokensford f. 41). Res. before 9 July 1339 (*Reg. R. de Salopia* I 359).

M. **John de Carleton** D.C.L. 1339–1349.
Coll. 9 July 1339 (*Reg. R. de Salopia* I 359). Exch. preb. with Gilbert de Bruer for preb. of Compton Bishop c. 29 Apr. 1349 (*CPP.* I 157).

M. **Gilbert de Bruer** 1349–1351.
By exch. Apr. 1349. Res. c. 14 July 1351 (*CPL.* III 430).

John de Horsington 1351, 1381/2.
Adam de Hertyndon 1367–?
William de Ferriby ?–1371.
Peter de Barton 1379.
Horsington prov. 14 July 1351 (*CPL.* III 430). Royal gr. to Hertyndon 7 May 1367 (*CPR. 1364–1367* p. 390). Ferriby evidently claimed preb. since exch. Haselbere with Hertyndon for preb. in Exeter, 6 Nov. 1371 and res. claims to Haselere (Exeter, Reg. Brantyngham II ii f. 17b). Barton occ. as preb. 22 Feb. 1379 (*Cal. MSS. D. & C. Wells* I 282), but Horsington called preb. of Haselbere at d., Sept. 1381/2 (*ibid.* II 17).

M. **John Manneston** ?–1401.
D. as preb. before 7 May 1401 (*CPR. 1399–1401* p. 445).

Henry Merston 1401–?
Royal gr. 7 May 1401 (*CPR. 1399–1401* p. 445).

William Marston 1402.
Occ. 18 Apr. 1402 (*Reg. Giffard and Bowet* p. 29).

Richard Aldryngton 1406, 1416.
Occ. 8 Sept. 1406 (*Reg. Giffard and Bowet* p. 60) and 10 July 1416 (*Reg. Bubwith* I 243).

Nicholas Sturgeon 1429–1440.
Coll. 28 Dec. 1429 (*Reg. Stafford (Bath and Wells)* I 75). Exch. preb. with Richard Betty for preb. of Reculversland, St Paul's, London, 6 Nov. 1440 (*ibid.* II 259).

M. **Richard Betty** B.C.L. 1440–1441.
By exch. Nov. 1440. D. before 18 Apr. 1441 (*Reg. Stafford (Bath and Wells)* II 270).

John Stopynton 1441–1447.
Coll. 18 Apr. 1441 (*Reg. Stafford (Bath and Wells)* II 270). D. before 18 May 1447 (*Reg. Bekynton* I 75).

M. **Robert Tarry** B.C.L. 1447–?
Coll. 18 May 1447 (*Reg. Bekynton* I 75). Occ. 1457/8 (*Cal. MSS. D. & C. Wells* II 89).

M. **William Bolton** B.C.L. 1477–?
Coll. 23 June 1477 (*Reg. Stillington* p. 111). ? Held preb. until d. before Aug. 1489 (Salis., Reg. Langton pt. i f. 26b).

M. **Thomas Beaumont** D.Cn. & C.L. 1501–1502.
Adm. 10 July 1501 (*Cal. MSS. D. & C. Wells* II 162). Archdcn. of Wells 1502.

M. **John Mertok** 1502–1503.
Adm. 19 Nov. 1502 (*Cal. MSS. D. & C. Wells* II 169). Res. before 4 Aug. 1503 (*Reg. King* p. 83).

M. **Alexander Hody** B.Cn.L. 1503–1519.
Coll. 4 Aug. 1503 (*Reg. King* p. 83). Adm. 14 Aug. (*Cal. MSS. D. & C. Wells* II 171). D. by Feb. 1519 (*Emden, Reg. Ox.* II 941).

M. **William Knight** D.C.L. ?–1541.
Occ. 1535 (*Valor* I 135). Bp. of Bath and Wells 1541.

Thomas Hobbys 1541–?
Royal gr. 1 Aug. 1541 (*L. & P.* XVI No. 1135 (2)).

PREBENDARIES OF HENSTRIDGE

M. **William de Kyngoscot** D.Cn.L. ?–1311.
D. as preb. before 19 Apr. 1311 (Reg. Drokensford f. 36).

Ivo de Berkeley 1311–1312.
Coll. 19 Apr. 1311 (Reg. Drokensford f. 36). Mand. by abp. 1 Apr. 1312, to revoke coll. (*ibid.* f. 43). Revoked 16 Apr. (*ibid.* f. 49).

M. **Gilbert de Middleton** 1312–?
Coll. by abp. 16 Apr. 1312 (Reg. Drokensford f. 49).

M. **Thomas de Garton** 1330–?
Royal gr. 5 May 1330 (*CPR. 1327–1330* p. 518).

Anibaldus Gaetani de Ceccano Card. pr. of S. Laurentius in Lucina. ?–1331.
Exch. preb. with Raymond Pelegrini for ch. of East Grinstead, Suss., 25 Aug. 1331 (*CPL.* II 328).

M. **Raymond Pelegrini** 1331–1352.
By exch. Aug. 1331. Estate ratif. 15 Jan. 1345 (*CPR. 1343–1345* p. 376). Exch. preb. with Henry de Walton for preb. in St Mary's by the castle colleg. ch., Leicester, 20 July 1352 (*Reg. R. de Salopia* II 696–7).

Henry de Walton 1352–?
By exch. July 1352. Adm. 2 Aug. (*Reg. R. de Salopia* II 697).

M. **Simon Thebaud de Sudbury** D.C.L. ?–1361.
Occ. as preb. 11 Nov. 1361 (*Cal. MSS. D. & C. Wells* I 266). Bp. of London, prov. 22 Oct., but cons. 20 March 1362.

John Thebaud de Sudbury 1361–1371.
Prov. 29 Dec. 1361 (*CPP.* I 384). Exch. preb. with Thomas de Sudbury for free chap. of St Mary the Virgin in the bp's palace, London, 31 Oct. 1371 (*Reg. Sudbury* I 35–6).

M. **Thomas Thebaud de Sudbury** 1371–?
By exch. Oct. 1371. Occ. 22 Feb. 1379 (*Cal. MSS. D. & C. Wells* I 283).

William de Odecumbe ?–1381/2.
D. as preb. Sept. 1381/2 (*Cal. MSS. D. & C. Wells* II 17).

E

Richard de Medeford 1386.
Royal gr. 11 July 1386 (*CPR. 1385–1389* p. 195).

M. Richard Clifford *senior* 1386–1400/1.
Royal gr. 13 Nov. 1386 (*CPR. 1385–1389* p. 236). Bp. of Bath and Wells 1400, k. refused to gr. temps. so probably Clifford held preb. until bp. of Worcester 1401.

Thomas de Stanley 1401–?
Royal gr. 1 Sept. 1401 (*CPR. 1399–1401* p. 536).

William Rosedefe 1405–?
Royal gr. 28 Nov. 1405 (*CPR. 1405–1408* p. 103).

William Skirwyth ?–1408.
Estate ratif. 30 Nov. 1407 (*CPR. 1405–1408* p. 369). Exch. preb. with John de Nottyngham for wardenship of St Mary Magdalen's hospital, Ripon, Yorks., 21 Oct. 1408 (*Reg. Bubwith* I 40).

John de Nottyngham 1408–1409.
By exch. Oct. 1408. Exch. preb. with Richard Kyngeston for preb. of St Mary's altar, Beverley colleg. ch., Yorks., 10 Feb. 1409 (*Reg. Bubwith* I 50).

Richard Kyngeston 1409–1418.
By exch. Feb. 1409. Coll. by bp. 1 March (*Reg. Bubwith* I 50). Mand. adm. 7 March (*Reg. Giffard and Bowet* p. 83). D. 14/24 Nov. 1418 (PCC 43 Marche; *Reg. Bubwith* II 347).

M. John Stokes Lic.C.L. 1418–1441.
Coll. 24 Nov. 1418 (*Reg. Bubwith* II 347). Exch. preb. with Nicholas Sturgeon for preb. in St Stephen's chap., Westminster, 14 Sept. 1441 (*Reg. Stafford* (*Bath and Wells*) II 272).

Nicholas Sturgeon 1441–1454.
By exch. Sept. 1441. D. 31 May/18 June 1454 (PCC 10 Rous).

M. John Pope D.Th. 1454–1457.
Coll. 30 Sept. 1454 (*Reg. Bekynton* I 239). Preb. of St Decumans 1457.

M. Thomas Merssh B.Cn. & C.L. 1457–1487.
Coll. 14 June 1457 (*Reg. Bekynton* I 286). D. 18 Jan./27 Feb. 1487 (PCC 1 Milles).

Thomas Botler 1487.
Adm. 3 May 1487 (*Cal. MSS. D. & C. Wells* II 104). Res. before 29 July (*ibid.* p. 106).

M. Thomas Gilbert D.Cn.L. 1487–1503.
Adm. 29 July 1487 (*Cal. MSS. D. & C. Wells* II 106). D. before 11 Aug. 1503 (*ibid.* p. 171).

M. Thomas Harris B.Cn.L. 1503–1511.
Adm. 29 Aug. 1503 (*Cal. MSS. D. & C. Wells* II 171–2). D. before 18 Feb. 1511 (*ibid.* pp. 226, 227).

M. John Fox 1511–1522.
Adm. 15 July 1511 (*Cal. MSS. D. & C. Wells* II 227). Exch. preb. with Richard Rawson for preb. in St Stephen's chap., Westminster, 1 July 1522 (*Reg. Bps., 1518–1559* p. 34).

M. **Richard**[1] **Rawson** 1522–?

By exch. July 1522. Occ. 12 Aug. 1538 (*Cal. MSS. D. & C. Wells* II 249). Probably held preb. until d. before 29 Oct. 1543 (Lond., Guildhall, Reg. Bonner f. 145).

PREBENDARIES OF HOLCOMBE

M. **Adam de Murymuth** D.C.L. ?–1340.

Res. this preb. before 20 May 1340 (*Reg. R. de Salopia* I 368).

Thomas de Murymuth 1340–?

Coll. 20 May 1340 (*Reg. R. de Salopia* I 368).

Walter de Boggeworth ?–1350.

D. as preb. before 24 Aug. 1350 (Exeter, Reg. Grandisson III f. 93).

M. **Thomas de Bukton** D.C.L. 1350–1354.

Adm. 24 Aug. 1350 (Exeter, Reg. Grandisson III f. 93). Petition for papal conf. 8 May 1352 (*CPP.* I 226). Exch. with Reginald de Bugwell for preb. of North Leverton, Southwell colleg. ch., Notts., 7 Oct. 1354 (York, Reg. Thoresby f. 92).

M. **Reginald de Bugwell** B.Cn. & C.L. 1354–?

By exch. Oct. 1354.

Walter de Alderbury 1360–1361.

Walter Moryn 1360–1361.

Alderbury adm. 27 May 1360 (Exeter, Reg. Grandisson III ff. 120b–121). Moryn prov. 14 Aug. (*CPP.* I 316). Alderbury probably res. before Aug. 1361 when adm. to preb. of Combe Quartadecima (*Cal. MSS. D. & C. Wells* I 263). Moryn d. before 28 Sept. (*CPP.* I 322).

Nicholas de Pontesbury 1361–1372.

Richard Bokelly 1367.

Pontesbury adm. 5 Oct. 1361 (Exeter, Reg. Grandisson III f. 128b). Royal gr. to Bokelly 19 Oct. 1367 (*CPR. 1367–1370* p. 23). Pontesbury retained possession, d. as preb. before 24 Oct. 1372 (Exeter, Reg. Brantyngham I f. 21).

John Grene 1372–?

Coll. 24 Oct. 1372 (Exeter, Reg. Brantyngham I f. 21). Mand. adm. 29 Oct. (*ibid.*).

Adam Akum ?–1377.

Exch. preb. with John Hope for bursal preb. in Crediton colleg. ch., Devon, 29 Nov. 1377 (Exeter, Reg. Brantyngham II i ff. 52–52b).

John Hope 1377–1391/2.

By exch. Nov. 1377. D. Sept. 1391/2 (*Cal. MSS. D. & C. Wells* II 21).

John Erghum ?–1392.

Exch. preb. and ch. of Upway, Dors., with Roger Tebrightone for ch. of Lympsham, Som., 21 Aug. 1392 (Salis., Reg. Waltham f. 144b). John Arum, possibly the same man, occ. 1391/2 (*Cal. MSS. D. & C. Wells* II 21).

Roger Tebrightone 1392–1393.

By exch. Aug. 1392. Mand. adm. 18 Oct. (Exeter, Reg. Brantyngham II i f. 138b). Exch. preb. with Thomas Maddynglee for preb. in Westbury-on-Trym colleg. ch., Glos., 22 Aug. 1393 (Worcester, Reg. Wakefield f. 108).

Thomas Maddynglee 1393–?

By exch. Aug. 1393. Adm. 16 Sept. (Exeter, Reg. Brantyngham II i ff. 144–144b).

[1] He is called Ralph Rawson 25 Dec. 1530 (*Reg. Bps., 1518–1559* p. 61), but this must be a scribal error.

M. John Orum D.Th. ?–1431.
Estate ratif. 23 Jan. 1408 (*CPR. 1405–1408* p. 369). Res. before 31 Jan. 1431 (*Reg. Stafford (Bath and Wells)* 1 95).

M. John Bernard B.Cn.L. 1431–1444.
Coll. 31 Jan. 1431 (*Reg. Stafford (Bath and Wells)* 1 95). Preb. of Wormenstre 1444.

John Trevenaunt 1444–1447.
Coll. 13 Feb. 1444 (*Reg. Bekynton* 1 7). Preb. of Wedmore Secunda 1447.

John Boleyn 1447–1448.
Coll. 21 Dec. 1447 (*Reg. Bekynton* 1 85). Vac. preb. before 1 Dec. 1448 (*ibid.* p. 107).

M. John Spekyngton M.A. 1448–1454.
Coll. 1 Dec. 1448 (*Reg. Bekynton* 1 107). Preb. of Combe Tercia 1454.

M. Thomas Chaundeler B.Th. 1454–1458.
Coll. 9 Oct. 1454 (*Reg. Bekynton* 1 240). Preb. of Combe Decima 1458.

M. Henry Abyndon B.Mus. 1458–1497.
Coll. 15 March 1458 (*Reg. Bekynton* 1 300). D. before 29 Aug. 1497 (Reg. King f. 10).

M. John Argentyne D.Th., D.M. 1497–1500.
Coll. 29 Aug. 1497 (Reg. King f. 10). Adm. 10 Sept. (*Cal. MSS. D. & C. Wells* II 147). Preb. of Combe Secunda 1500.

M. Robert Widewe B.Mus. 1500–1505.
Coll. 25 May 1500 (*Reg. King* p. 49). D. before 5 Oct. 1505 (*Cal. MSS. D. & C. Wells* II 184).

John Hans 1505–1509.
Adm. 5 Oct. 1505 (*Cal. MSS. D. & C. Wells* II 184). D. before 8 Feb. 1509 (*ibid.* p. 211).

M. Reginald West 1509–?
Adm. 8 Feb. 1509 (*Cal. MSS. D. & C. Wells* II 211). ? Held preb. until d. 22 Feb./ 6 March 1516 (*Som. Med. Wills 1501–1530* pp. 183–6).

M. Thomas Stephens D.Th. ?–1520/1.
D. as preb. Sept. 1520/1 (*Cal. MSS. D. & C. Wells* II 240).

M. William Piers D.C.L. 1529, 1535.
Occ. 15 Oct. 1529 (Exeter, Reg. Veysey 1 f. 45). Occ. 1535 (*Valor* 1 135).

PREBENDARIES OF HUISH AND BRENT

This prebend was attached to the archdeaconry of Wells.

PREBENDARIES OF ILMINSTER

Note : This prebend was held by the abbots of Muchelney.

Ralph de Muchelney O.S.B. 1294–1305.
Lic. el. sought 15 June 1294 (P.R.O., C 84/12/8), gr. 19 June (*CPR. 1292–1301* p. 74). Petition for royal assent 25 June (P.R.O., C 84/12/12), gr. 3 July (*CPR. 1292–1301* p. 78). Temps. 5 Aug. (*ibid.* p. 83). D. before 19 Jan. 1305 (*CPR. 1301–1307* p. 310).

John de Henton O.S.B. 1305–1334.

Lic. el. gr. 19 Jan. 1305 (*CPR. 1301–1307* p. 310). Petition for royal assent 3 Feb. (P.R.O., C 84/15/26), gr. 1 March (*CPR. 1301–1307* p. 315). Temps. 10 Apr. (*ibid.* p. 328). D. before 14 June 1334 (P.R.O., C 84/23/10).

John de Somertone O.S.B. 1334–1347.

Lic. el. sought 14 June 1334 (P.R.O., C 84/23/10), gr. 21 June (*CPR. 1330–1334* p. 551). El. notified to k. 2 July (P.R.O., C 84/23/11). Royal assent 8 July (*CPR. 1330–1334* p. 559). El. conf. by bp. 19 July (*Reg. R. de Salopia* I 173). Temps. 24 July (*CPR. 1330–1334* p. 567). D. before 9 Sept. 1347 (*CPR. 1345–1348* p. 375).

John de Codeworth O.S.B. 1347–1349.

Lic. el. gr. 9 Sept. 1347 (*CPR. 1345–1348* p. 375). Royal assent 17 Sept. (*ibid.* p. 403). Temps. 1 Nov. (*ibid.* p. 424). D. before 22 May 1349 (*CPR. 1348–1350* p. 293).

Thomas de Overtone O.S.B. 1349–1370.

Lic. el. gr. 22 May 1349 (*CPR. 1348–1350* p. 293). Royal assent 29 May (*ibid.* p. 295). Temps. 16 June (*ibid.* p. 306). D. 17 Nov. 1370 (P.R.O., C 84/30/35).

William de Schepton O.S.B. 1370–1398.

Lic. el. sought 18 Nov. 1370 (P.R.O., C 84/30/35), gr. 21 Nov. (*CPR. 1370–1374* p. 13). Royal assent 1 Dec. (*ibid.* p. 23). Temps. 19 Dec. (*ibid.* p. 28). D. before 20 Feb. 1398 (P.R.O., C 84/37/13).

Nicholas Stratton O.S.B. 1398–1400.

Lic. el. sought 20 Feb. 1398 (P.R.O., C 84/37/13), gr. 23 Feb. (*CPR. 1396–1399* p. 276). Royal assent 6 March (*ibid.* p. 315). Temps. 19 March (*ibid.* p. 316). D. before 20 Aug. 1400 (*CPR. 1399–1401* p. 332).

John de Bruton O.S.B. 1400–1432.

Lic. el. gr. 20 Aug. 1400 (*CPR. 1399–1401* p. 332). Temps. 13 Sept. (*ibid.* p. 333). D. before 30 March 1432 (P.R.O., C 84/44/17).

John Cherde O.S.B. 1432–1463.

Lic. el. sought 30 March 1432 (P.R.O., C 84/44/17). El. notified to k. 10 Apr. (P.R.O., C 84/44/19). Royal assent 15 Apr. (*CPR. 1429–1436* p. 190). Temps. 28 Apr. (*ibid.*). D. 10 Sept. 1463 (*Reg. Bekynton* II 463).

Thomas Pipe O.S.B. 1463–1465.

Lic. el. gr. 13 Sept. 1463 (*CPR. 1461–1467* p. 285). El. 20 Sept. (*Reg. Bekynton* II 463). Royal assent 24 Sept. (*CPR. 1461–1467* p. 285). Conf. by bp. 13 Oct. (*Reg. Bekynton* II 465). Profession to bp. and mand. adm. to preb. of Ilminster s.d. (*ibid.*). D. before 25 June 1465 (*CPR. 1461–1467* p. 457).

William Crukerne O.S.B. 1465–1471.

Lic. el. gr. 25 June 1465 (*CPR. 1461–1467* p. 457). Temps. 23 July (*ibid.*). D. before 18 March 1471 (P.R.O., C 84/50/6).

John Bracy O.S.B. 1471–1490.

Lic. el. sought 18 March 1471 (P.R.O., C 84/50/6), gr. 21 March (*CPR. 1467–1477* p. 239). El. notified to k. 4 Apr. (P.R.O., C 84/50/8). Royal assent 7 Apr. (*CPR. 1467–1477* p. 239). Temps. 16 July (*ibid.* p. 266). D. before 27 May 1490 (*CPR. 1485–1494* p. 311).

William Wyke O.S.B. 1490–1504.

Lic. el. gr. 27 May 1490 (*CPR. 1485–1494* p. 311). Royal assent 20 June (*ibid.*). Temps. 4 July (*ibid.* p. 315). Adm. to preb. of Ilminster 20 June 1491 (*Cal. MSS. D. & C. Wells* II 122). D. before 29 Oct. 1504 (*CPR. 1494–1509* p. 393).

Thomas Broke O.S.B. 1504–1522.
Lic. el. gr. 29 Oct. 1504 (*CPR. 1494–1509* p. 393). Royal assent 4 Dec. (*ibid.*). El. conf. by bp. 21 Jan. 1505 (*Reg. King* p. 189). D. before 5 Sept. 1522 (*L. & P.* III ii No. 2563).

John Shirborn O.S.B. 1522–1532.
Lic. el. sought 5 Sept. 1522 (*L. & P.* III ii No. 2563), gr. 23 Sept. (*ibid.*). Petition for royal assent 12 Oct. (*ibid.* No. 2610). Temps. 12 Nov. (*ibid.* No. 2668). D. before 7 Aug. 1532 (*ibid.* v No. 1270 (7)).

Thomas Ine O.S.B. 1532–1538.
Lic. el. sought 7 Aug. 1532 (*L. & P.* v No. 1270 (7)), gr. 19 Aug. (*ibid.*). Royal assent 2 Sept. (*ibid.* No. 1370 (11)). Temps. 8 Oct. (*ibid.* No. 1499 (16)). Abbot at time of surrender of abbey 3 Jan. 1538 (*ibid.* XIII i No. 27).

PREBENDARIES OF ILTON

William de Blibury ?–1313.
D. as preb. before 15 Feb. 1313 (*Reg. Drokensford* p. 151).

William de Hanlo 1313–1319.
Coll. 15 Feb. 1313 (*Reg. Drokensford* p. 151). D. before 12 Feb. 1319 (*ibid.* p. 21).

Gaillard de la Motte Card. dcn. of S. Lucia in Orthea. 1320.

Geoffrey *or* **Gilbert de Exton** *or* **de Eyton** 1319–1328.
Exton coll. 24 March 1319 (*Reg. Drokensford* p. 132). Comm. 25 March to remove intruder from preb. and gr. possession to Exton (*ibid.*). ? Intruder card. Gaillard, since bp. sent mand. 6 Nov. 1320 to card. that he had waited more than one month before collating Exton to preb. held by Hanlo and card. no longer able to claim preb. (*ibid.* p. 183). Exton d. as preb. before 1 Jan. 1328 (*ibid.* p. 279).

Thomas de Drokensford 1328–?
Coll. 1 Jan. 1328 (*Reg. Drokensford* p. 279).

M. **Henry de Idesworth** 1329–?
David Maynard ?–1339.
Royal gr. to Idesworth 6 Oct. 1329 (*CPR. 1327–1330* p. 447). Coll. 12 Oct. (*Reg. R. de Salopia* I 9). Maynard claimed preb. as had been prov. to canonry at Wells with expectation of preb. 18 Aug. 1327 (*CPL.* II 261). Mand. from bp. to Maynard 15 Dec. 1336 that he should produce title to preb. (*Reg. R. de Salopia* I 315). Obtained possession of preb. since bp. cited by official of abp. of Canterbury 12 June 1338, because claimed that Maynard not in orders (*ibid.* p. 323). Res. before 7 Aug. 1339 (*ibid.* p. 359).

M. **John de Ildesleigh** B.Cn.L. 1339–?
Coll. 7 Aug. 1339 (*Reg. R. de Salopia* I 359).

Stephen de Brokesbourne 1351.
Estate ratif. 6 Oct. 1351 (*CPR. 1350–1354* p. 150).

Thomas de Bockyng 1366.
Occ. Sept. 1366 (*Reg. Langham* p. 65).[1]

Thomas Maddynglee 1370–?
Royal gr. 29 Nov. 1370 (*CPR. 1370–1374* p. 21).

---

[1] Bockyng occ. as can. of Wells 1377 (P.R.O., E 179/4/1).

Nicholas Bubwith 1399.
Estate ratif. 14 Oct. 1399 (*CPR. 1399–1401* p. 4).

M. John Colles 1405, 1406.
Occ. 9 Apr. 1405 (*Reg. Giffard and Bowet* p. 55). Estate ratif. 17 Apr. 1406 (*CPR. 1405–1408* p. 244). ? Held preb. until d. by Oct. 1418 (Salis., Reg. Chaundeler pt. i f. 12).

M. Thomas Stephens Lic.C.L. 1418–1420.
Coll. 25 Oct. 1418 (*Reg. Bubwith* II 338). D. before 7 July 1420 (*ibid.* p. 392).

John Reynold 1420–1450.
Coll. 7 July 1420 (*Reg. Bubwith* II 392). D. before 9 Apr. 1450 (*Reg. Bekynton* I 144).

M. Thomas Purveour M.A. 1450–1451.
Coll. 14 Apr. 1450 (*Reg. Bekynton* I 144–5). Preb. of Yatton 1451.

M. William Say B.Th. 1451–1464.
Coll. 3 Oct. 1451 (*Reg. Bekynton* I 171). Res. before 2 Aug. 1464 (*ibid.* p. 418).

M. John Chedworth D.C.L. 1464–1472.
M. William Witham D.C.L. 1467.
Chedworth coll. 2 Aug. 1464 (*Reg. Bekynton* I 418). Witham occ. as preb. 28 Aug. 1467 (*Reg. Stillington* p. 11), but probably a scribal error since he occ. as dn. in July. Chedworth d. as preb. before 7 Jan. 1472 (*ibid.* p. 90).

M. William Nykke 1472–1473.
Coll. 12 Apr. 1472 (*Reg. Stillington* p. 90). Archdcn. of Wells 1473.

Robert Stillington 1473–?
Coll. 12 Apr. 1473 (*Reg. Stillington* p. 96). Occ. 27 May 1486 (*ibid.* p. 138).

M. William Cosyn Lic.C.L. 1498.
Adm. 28 Oct. 1498 (*Cal. MSS. D. & C. Wells* II 153). Dean in Dec.

M. John Pikman B.C.L. 1499–1503.
Adm. 31 March 1499 (*Cal. MSS. D. & C. Wells* II 155). D. 6 Feb./15 March 1503 (*Som. Med. Wills 1501–1530* p. 39).

M. George Percy B.Cn.L. 1503–1506.
Adm. 27 May 1503 (*Cal. MSS. D. & C. Wells* II 171). Res. before 9 Dec. 1506 (*ibid.* p. 199).

M. Thomas Wellis D.Th. 1506–1524.
Adm. 9 Dec. 1506 (*Cal. MSS. D. & C. Wells* II 199). D. before Sept. 1524 (*ibid.* p. 241).

Robert Fryer 1535.
Occ. 1535 (*Valor* I 135).

PREBENDARIES OF LITTON

Bartholomew Tirel ?–1345.
Exch. preb. with Richard de Rodeneye for preb. of Cudworth, 13 Jan. 1345 (*Reg. R. de Salopia* II 522).

Richard de Rodeneye 1345–?
By exch. Jan. 1345.

John de Blebury 1363-1366.
Royal gr. 28 Oct. 1363 (*CPR. 1361-1364* p. 405). Exch. preb. with John de Crykke-lade for portion of tithes of Nuthanger, Kingsclere, Hants, 28 Oct. 1366 (*Cal. MSS. D. & C. Wells* I 269).

John de Crykkelade 1366-?
By exch. Oct. 1366.

Richard Harewell 1366-1435.
Adm. 1 Oct. 1366[1] (*Cal. MSS. D. & C. Wells* I 293). D. before 15 May 1435 (*Reg. Stafford (Bath and Wells)* II 183).

M. John Storthwayt B.C.L. 1435-1452.
Coll. 15 May 1435 (*Reg. Stafford (Bath and Wells)* II 183). D. before 2 Feb. 1452 (*Reg. Bekynton* I 177).

Richard Hayman 1452-1464.
Coll. 2 Feb. 1452 (*Reg. Bekynton* I 177). D. before 3 Oct. 1464 (*ibid.* p. 421).

M. Hugh Sugar *or* Norris D.C.L. 1464-1489.
Coll. 3 Oct. 1464 (*Reg. Bekynton* I 421). D. before 5 May 1489 (PCC 23 Milles).

M. Oliver Dynham M.A. 1489-1500.
Coll. 25 May 1489 (*Reg. Stillington* p. 158). Adm. 29 May (*Cal. MSS. D. & C. Wells* II 115). D. 2 Apr./30 May 1500 (PCC 9 Moone).

Edward Bray 1500-1503.
Adm. 3 Aug. 1500 (*Cal. MSS. D. & C. Wells* II 159). Vac. preb. by 30 May 1503 (*ibid.* p. 171).

John Bray 1503-?
Coll. 30 May 1503 (*Cal. MSS. D. & C. Wells* II 171).

M. William Bennet D.C.L. ?-1533.
M. Thomas Winter 1526.
Bennet occ. 1523 (*Reg. Bps., 1518-1559* pp. 76, 77, 78). Winter occ. 26 March 1526 (*L. & P.* IV i No. 2054). Bennet d. in possession of preb. before 5 Oct. 1533. (Lond., Guildhall, Reg. Stokesley f. 20; PCC 14 Hogen).

M. Thomas Bedell B.C.L. 1533, 1535.
Occ. 1533 (*L. & P.* VI No. 1594). Occ. 1535 (*Valor* I 134). ? Held preb. until d. by Sept. 1537 (*L. & P.* XII ii No. 646).

PREBENDARIES OF LONG SUTTON

Note: This prebend was held by the abbots of Athelney.

Andrew de Sancto *or* Sacro Fonte O.S.B. 1280-1300.
Royal assent to el. 14 March 1280 (*CPR. 1272-1281* p. 366). Temps. 29 Apr. (*ibid.* p. 368). D. before 1 Apr. 1300 (P.R.O., C 84/13/44).

Osmund de Sowi O.S.B. 1300-1325.
Lic. el. sought 1 Apr. 1300 (P.R.O., C 84/13/44), gr. 5 Apr. (*CPR. 1292-1301* p. 503). Royal assent 19 Apr. (*ibid.* p. 510). Temps. 13 May (*ibid.* p. 513). D. before 19 Jan. 1325 (*CPR. 1324-1327* p. 86).

---

[1] There is probably an error about the year of Harewell's adm. to the preb. since the entry occ. as a memorandum among entries relating to the year 1382 and is written in a different hand (Reg. 1 f. 285b). There is no record of a law suit between Harewell and Blebury who exch. the preb. with Crykkelade, 28 Oct. 1366, apparently after the date of Harewell's adm.

Robert de Ile O.S.B. 1325–1341.

Lic. el. gr. 19 Jan. 1325 (*CPR. 1324–1327* p. 86). Petition for royal assent 7 Feb. (P.R.O., C 84/20/46), gr. 13 Feb. (*CPR. 1324–1327* p. 88). Temps. 16 March (*ibid.* p. 109). Profession to bp. 25 March (*Reg. Drokensford* p. 243). D. before 26 June 1341 (P.R.O., C 84/24/20).

Richard de Gothurst O.S.B. 1341–1349.

Lic. el. sought 26 June 1341 (P.R.O., C 84/24/20), gr. 2 Aug. (*CPR. 1340–1343* p. 253). Royal assent 20 Aug. (*ibid.* p. 278). Temps. 4 Sept. (*ibid.* p. 282). D. before 19 Sept. 1349 (P.R.O., C 84/26/21).

John de Stoure O.S.B. 1349.

Lic. el. sought 19 Sept. 1349 (P.R.O., C 84/26/21), gr. 23 Sept. (*CPR. 1348–1350* p. 376). D. before 6 Oct. (P.R.O., C 84/26/28).

Robert de Hache O.S.B. 1349–1390.

Lic. el. sought 6 Oct. 1349 (P.R.O., C 84/26/28), gr. 10 Oct. (*CPR. 1348–1350* p. 395). Royal assent 22 Oct. (*ibid.* p. 410). Temps. 5 Nov. (*ibid.* p. 419). D. before 5 Oct. 1390 (P.R.O., C 84/34/46).

John Hewish O.S.B. 1390–1399.

Lic. el. sought 5 Oct. 1390 (P.R.O., C 84/34/46), gr. 7 Oct. (*CPR. 1388–1392* p. 307). Royal assent 18 Oct. (*ibid.* p. 312). Temps. 2 Nov. (*ibid.* p. 318). Instal. as preb. of Long Sutton 4 Aug. 1391 (*Cal. MSS. D. & C. Wells* I 303). D. before 11 June 1399 (P.R.O., C 84/37/43).

John Brigge O.S.B. 1399–1424.

Lic. el. sought 11 June 1399 (P.R.O., C 84/37/43), gr. 16 June (*CPR. 1396–1399* p. 578). Royal assent 24 June (*ibid.* p. 587). Temps. 10 July (*ibid.* p. 588). D. before 13 Nov. 1424 (*CPR. 1422–1429* p. 254).

John Petherton O.S.B. 1424–1458.

Lic. el. gr. 13 Nov. 1424 (*CPR. 1422–1429* p. 254). Royal assent 28 Nov. (*ibid.* p. 256). Temps. 10 Dec. (*ibid.* p. 262). D. 10 Feb. 1458 (*Reg. Bekynton* II 459).

Robert Hylle O.S.B. 1458–1485.

Lic. el. gr. 15 Feb. 1458 (*CPR. 1452–1461* p. 417). El. 27 Feb. (*Reg. Bekynton* II 460). Royal assent 4 March (*CPR. 1452–1461* p. 417). Conf. by bp. 11 March (*Reg. Bekynton* II 459). Profession to bp. s.d. (*ibid.*). Temps. 14 March (*CPR. 1452–1461* p. 418). D. before 16 Oct. 1485 (*CPR. 1485–1494* p. 19).

John George O.S.B. 1485–1503.

Lic. el. gr. 16 Oct. 1485 (*CPR. 1485–1494* p. 19). Royal assent 4 Nov. (*ibid.* p. 33). Temps. 23 Nov. (*ibid.* p. 34). D. before 26 May 1503 (*CPR. 1494–1509* p. 303).

John Wellington O.S.B. 1503–1516.

Lic. el. gr. 26 May 1503 (*CPR. 1494–1509* p. 303). Adm. to preb. of Long Sutton 8 Aug. (*Cal. MSS. D. & C. Wells* II 171). Temps. 1 Feb. 1504 (*CPR. 1494–1509* p. 371). D. before 5 Nov. 1516 (*L. & P.* II i No. 2581).

Richard Wraxall *or* **Bele** O.S.B. 1516–1518.

Lic. el. sought 5 Nov. 1516 (*L. & P.* II i No. 2581), gr. 8 Nov. (*ibid.*). Royal assent sought 2 Dec. (*ibid.* No. 2664), gr. 12 Dec. (*ibid.*). El. conf. by bp. 7 Jan. 1517 (*Reg. King* p. 190). Profession to bp. 8 Jan. (*ibid.*). Mand. adm. to preb. of Long Sutton 16 Jan. (*ibid.* p. 191). Temps. 31 Jan. (*L. & P.* II ii No. 2852). D. before 27 March 1518 (*ibid.* No. 4036).

John Herte O.S.B. 1518–1527.
Lic. el. gr. 27 March 1518 (*L. & P.* II ii No. 4036). Royal assent 12 Apr. (*ibid.* No. 4078). Temps. 20 Apr. (*ibid.*). D. before 19 Feb. 1527 (*ibid.* IV ii No. 2901).

Thomas Sutton O.S.B. 1527–1531.
Lic. el. gr. 19 Feb. 1527 (*L. & P.* IV ii No. 2901). Petition for royal assent 7 Apr.—appointment had been made by card. abp. of York to whom abbey had delegated rights (*ibid.* No. 3027). Petition by card. abp. for temps. (*ibid.* No. 3037). D. before 3 Feb. 1531 (*ibid.* V No. 119 (66)).

John Maior O.S.B. 1531–1533.
Lic. el. sought 3 Feb. 1531 (*L. & P.* V No. 119 (66)), gr. 22 Feb. (*ibid.*). Petition for royal assent 18 March (*ibid.* No. 166 (55)). Temps. 16 July (*ibid.* No. 364 (31)). D. before 24 Feb. 1533 (*ibid.* VI No. 264).

Robert Hamlyn O.S.B. 1533–1539.
Lic. el. sought 24 Feb. 1533 (*L. & P.* VI No. 264), gr. 22 March (*ibid.*). Petition for royal assent 14 June (*ibid.* No. 737 (18)), gr. 22 June (*ibid.*). Temps. 20 Nov. (*ibid.* No. 1481 (20)). Abbot at time of surrender of the abbey 8 Feb. 1539 (*L. & P.* XIV i No. 254).

PREBENDARIES OF MILVERTON PRIMA

This prebend was attached to the archdeaconry of Taunton.

PREBENDARIES OF MILVERTON SECUNDA

John Auger ?–1375.
Occ. 18 Nov. 1366 (*Reg. Langham* p. 68). Estate ratif. 18 Oct. 1373 (*CPR. 1370–1374* p. 348). D. before 25 Dec. 1375 (*Cal. MSS. D. & C. Wells* I 277).

John Grene ?–1410.
Occ. 12 Feb. 1379 (*Cal. MSS. D. & C. Wells* I 282). D. 2/12 Jan. 1410 (PCC 32 Marche; *Reg. Bubwith* I 69–70).

M. John Tyssebury B.C.L. 1410–1413.
Coll. 12 Jan. 1410 (*Reg. Bubwith* I 69–70). D. 2/8 May 1413 (PCC 26 Marche; *Reg. Bubwith* I 143).

Stephen Morpath 1413–1449.
Coll. 8 May 1413 (*Reg. Bubwith* I 143). Preb. of Compton Dundon 1449.

M. John Stokes B.Cn. & C.L. 1449–1479.
Coll. 24 March 1449 (*Reg. Bekynton* I 111). D. before 15 July 1479 (*Reg. Stillington* p. 114).

M. John Austell B.Cn. & C.L. 1479–1498/9.
Coll. 15 July 1479 (*Reg. Stillington* p. 114). D. 17 Dec. 1498/15 Feb. 1499 (PCC 29 Horne).

M. Stephen Dowce B.Th. 1499–1518/19.
Adm. 30 March 1499 (*Cal. MSS. D. & C. Wells* II 155). D. Sept. 1518/19 (*ibid.* p. 240).

John Algar 1535.
Occ. 1535 (*Valor* I 137).

PREBENDARIES OF NORTH CURRY

Thomas de Beauford 1349–?
William de Saxeby 1349.
Royal gr. to Beauford 33 (*sic*) Apr. 1349 (*CPR. 1348–1350* p. 287). Mand. adm. 23 Apr. (*Reg. R. de Salopia* II 610). Saxeby had been prov. to canonry in Wells with expectation of preb. 9 May 1343 (*CPL.* III 60) and claimed North Curry 1349. Royal mand. 12 Oct. that bp. to adm. fit person to preb. as k. had recovered pres. to preb. against Saxeby (*Reg. R. de Salopia* II 617).

William de Odecumbe ?–1362.
Res. this preb. 22 Apr. 1362 when coll. to preb. of Wedmore Quarta (*Reg. R. de Salopia* II 762).

Roger Tebrightone 1362–?
Coll. 24 Apr. 1362 (*Reg. R. de Salopia* II 763). Occ. 22 Feb. and 4 March 1379 (*Cal. MSS. D. & C. Wells* I 283, 284). ? Held preb. until 1392 when preb. of Holcombe.

William Calf ?–1419.
D. as preb. before 18 Sept. 1419 (*Reg. Bubwith* II 374).

M. **John Stone** Sch.Th. 1419–?
Coll. 18 Sept. 1419 (*Reg. Bubwith* II 374).

Roger Coryndon 1427–1432.
Coll. 12 March 1427 (*Reg. Stafford (Bath and Wells)* I 45). Res. before 5 June 1432 (*ibid.* p. 121).

M. **William Bykonill** B.C.L. 1432–1443.
Coll. 5 June 1432 (*Reg. Stafford (Bath and Wells)* I 121). Preb. of Dultingcote 1443.

M. **William Fulford** B.Cn. & C.L. 1443–1452.
Mand. adm. 15 Sept. 1443 (Lamb., Reg. Stafford f. 9). Preb. of Cudworth 1452.

M. **Thomas Merssh** B.Cn. & C.L. 1452–1453.
Coll. 28 May 1452 (*Reg. Bekynton* I 185). Preb. of Wedmore Quarta 1453.

M. **Robert Peuesy** B.Cn. & C.L. 1453–1459.
Coll. 31 May 1453 (*Reg. Bekynton* I 206). Preb. of Wedmore Quarta 1459.

M. **Richard Lichefeld** D.C.L. 1459–1460.
Coll. 6 Aug. 1459 (*Reg. Bekynton* I 327). Archdcn. of Bath 1460.

M. **John Colville** ?–1472.
D. as preb. before 13 Jan. 1472 (*Reg. Stillington* p. 90).

M. **Robert Newbald** B.Cn. & C.L. 1472–1473.
Coll. 13 Jan. 1472 (*Reg. Stillington* p. 90). D. before 15 July 1473 (*ibid.* p. 100).

M. **John Austell** B.Cn. & C.L. 1473–?
Coll. 15 July 1473 (*Reg. Stillington* p. 100). ? Res. 1479 when preb. of Milverton Secunda.

John Stephens 1488–?
Adm. 30 Jan. 1488 (*Cal. MSS. D. & C. Wells* II 110).

M. Robert Dyker B.Cn. & C.L. 1504–1532.
Royal gr. 28 Sept. 1504 (*CPR. 1494–1509* p. 384). Adm. 5 Oct. (*Cal. MSS. D. & C Wells* II 178). D. 17/24 July 1532 (PCC 16 Thower).

M. John Gudman B.Cn.L. ?–1548.
Occ. 1535 (*Valor* I 134). Dean 1548.

PREBENDARIES OF PILTON

Note : This prebend was held by the abbots of Glastonbury.

John de Kantia O.S.B. 1291–1303.
Lic. el. sought 5 Oct. 1291 (P.R.O., C 84/10/22), gr. 8 Oct. (*CPR. 1281–1292* p. 447). Notified to k. 18 Oct. (P.R.O., C 84/10/24). Royal assent 22 Oct. (*CPR. 1281–1292* p. 448). D. before 20 Dec. 1303 (P.R.O., C 84/15/6).

Geoffrey de Fromond O.S.B. 1303–1322.
Lic. el. sought 20 Dec. 1303 (P.R.O., C 84/15/6). Royal assent 18 Jan. 1304 (*CPR. 1301–1307* p. 205). Notification by bp. to k. that el. canonical 4 Feb. (P.R.O., C 84/15/8). Temps. 10 Feb. (*CPR. 1301–1307* p. 209). D. before 26 Nov. 1322 (*CPR. 1321–1324* p. 220).

Walter de Taunton O.S.B. 1322–1323.
Lic. el. gr. 26 Nov. 1322 (*CPR. 1321–1324* p. 220). Royal assent 20 Dec. (*ibid.* p. 229). D. before 27 Jan. 1323 (P.R.O., C 84/20/17)—before temps. had been restored.

Adam de Sudbury O.S.B. 1323–1334.
Lic. el. sought 27 Jan. 1323 (P.R.O., C 84/20/17). Royal assent to el. 16 Feb. (*CPR. 1321–1324* p. 241). Temps. 12 March (*ibid.* p. 265). D. 30 Oct. 1334 (P.R.O., C 84/23/29).

John de Breynton O.S.B. 1334–1342.
Lic. el. sought 30 Oct. 1334 (P.R.O., C 84/23/29), gr. 6 Nov. (*CPR. 1334–1338* p. 43). Petition for royal assent to el. 16 Nov. (P.R.O., C 84/23/19), gr. 20 Nov. (*CPR. 1334–1338* p. 47). Temps. 24 Dec. (*ibid.* p. 53). D. before 29 Sept. 1342 (*CPR. 1340–1343* p. 530).

Walter de Monyngton O.S.B. 1342–1375.
Lic. el. gr. 29 Sept. 1342 (*CPR. 1340–1343* p. 530). Royal assent 13 Oct. (*ibid.*). Conf. by bp. 25 Oct. (*Reg. R. de Salopia* II 454–5). Temps. 11 Nov. (*CPR. 1340–1343* p. 568). D. before 14 July 1375 (P.R.O., C 84/31/31).

John Chinnock O.S.B. 1375–1420.
Lic. el. sought 14 July 1375 (P.R.O., C 84/31/31), gr. 18 July (*CPR. 1374–1377* p. 128). El. notified to k. 25 July (P.R.O., C 84/31/32). Royal assent 1 Aug. (*CPR. 1374–1377* p. 132). Temps. 17 Aug. (*ibid.*). D. before 10 Aug. 1420 (*Reg. Bubwith* II 483).

M. Nicholas Frome O.S.B., D.Th. 1420–1456.
Lic. el. gr. 10 Aug. 1420 (*Reg. Bubwith* II 483). Royal assent 4 Sept. (*ibid.*). Conf. by bp. 19 Sept. (*ibid.* pp. 481–2). Mand. to install 23 Sept. (*ibid.* p. 483). D. before 30 Apr. 1456 (*CPR. 1452–1461* p. 281).

Walter More O.S.B. 1456.
Lic. el. gr. 30 Apr. 1456 (*CPR. 1452–1461* p. 281). Royal assent 13 May (*ibid.*). Temps. 26 May (*ibid.* p. 292). D. 22 Oct. (*Reg. Bekynton* II 450).

John Shelwood O.S.B. 1456–1493.

Lic. el. gr. 7 Nov. 1456 (*CPR. 1452–1461* p. 330). El. 13–15 Nov. (*Reg. Bekynton* II 450–3). Royal assent 24 Nov. (*CPR. 1452–1461* p. 330). El. conf. by bp. 29 Nov. (*Reg. Bekynton* II 450). Profession to bp. 30 Nov. (*ibid.* pp. 453–4). Temps. 7 Dec. (*CPR. 1452–1461* p. 331). D. before 14 July 1493 (*CPR. 1485–1494* p. 426).

M. Thomas Wasyn O.S.B., B.Th. 1493.

Lic. el. gr. 14 July 1493 (*CPR. 1485–1494* p. 426). El. annulled by bp. c. 12 Nov. (*Reg. Stillington* p. 200).

Richard Beere O.S.B. 1493–1525.

Appointed by bp. 12 Nov. 1493 (*Reg. Stillington* p. 200). Temps. 19 Nov. (*CPR. 1485–1494* p. 452). Profession to bp. 19 Jan. 1494 (*Reg. Stillington* p. 200). Instal. 20 Jan. (*ibid.*). D. 20 Jan. 1525 (*Reg. Bps., 1518–1559* p. 84).

Richard Whyting O.S.B. 1525–1539.

Lic. el. gr. 1 Feb. 1525 (*Reg. Bps., 1518–1559* p. 84). El. 16 Feb. (*ibid.*). Conf. by card. abp. of York 3 March (*ibid.* p. 86). Opposers of el. cited 23 March to appear 1 Apr. (*ibid.* p. 87). Royal assent 24 March (*ibid.*). Temps. 5 Apr. (*L. & P.* IV i No. 1244). Hanged 15 Nov. 1539 (*ibid.* XIV ii Nos. 530, 531).

PREBENDARIES OF ST DECUMANS

M. Robert de Gloucestre ?–1322.

Said to have held preb. during episcopates of bps. de Marcia and Haselschawe and during part of the episcopate of bp. Drokensford (*Reg. R. de Salopia* II 642). Probably held preb. from 1293 when de Marcia el. until d., before 31 Jan. 1322 (*Reg. A. de Orleton*, ed. A. T. Bannister (Canterbury and York Soc., v) p. 209).

John Giffard ?–1349.

Occ. 3 Feb. 1335 (*CPR. 1334–1338* p. 72). Estate ratif. 20 March (*ibid.*). Occ. 20 July 1349 (*Reg. R. de Salopia* II 611). D. before 17 Oct. (*CPP.* I 185).

Benjamin Bernard 1349.

M. Bernard Brocas 1349–1366.

M. Reginald de Bugwell B.Cn. & C.L. 1349.

Estate of Brocas ratif. 7 Oct. 1349 (*CPR. 1348–1350* p. 395). Bernard said to have held preb. 1349 before Brocas coll. (*Reg. R. de Salopia* II 642). Bugwell accepted prov. to preb. 9 Nov. (*CPP.* I 185). Royal prohibn., 10 Feb. 1350 against all ecclesiastical persons taking proceedings in derogation of k's right to collate to preb. (*CPR. 1348–1350* p. 526). Royal gr. to Brocas 26 Feb. (*ibid.* p. 475), second gr. 17 March (*Reg. R. de Salopia* II 631). Estate ratif. 3 July (*CPR. 1348–1350* p. 542). Exch. preb. with Arnald Brocas for chap. of Whipstrode St James, North Fareham, Hants, 18 Oct. 1366 (*Cal. MSS. D. & C. Wells* I 269).

M. Arnald Brocas 1366–?

By exch. Oct. 1366. Royal gr. 11 May 1367 (*CPR. 1364–1367* p. 389). Occ. 12 Feb. 1379 (*Cal. MSS. D. & C. Wells* I 282). ? Held preb. until d. before 20 Aug. 1395 (Linc., Reg. XI (Buckingham) f. 442).

M. Ralph Erghum ?–1410.

Estate ratif. 4 Oct. 1397 (*CPR. 1396–1399* p. 199) and 25 Sept. 1401 (*CPR. 1399–1401* p. 483). D. 3/8 March 1410 (PCC 21 Marche; *Reg. Bubwith* I 5).

M. **Thomas Bubwith** 1410–1419.
Coll. 8 March 1410 (*Reg. Bubwith* I 5, 75). Archdcn. of Wells 1419.

Thomas Shelford 1419–1426.
Coll. 14 Apr. 1419 (*Reg. Bubwith* II 356). D. before 4 Sept. 1426 (*Reg. Stafford* (*Bath and Wells*) I 41).

M. **David Price** D.C.L. ?–1433.
Occ. 15 Apr. 1428 (*Reg. Stafford* (*Bath and Wells*) I 61). Preb. of Ashill 1433.

John Hillier 1433–1435.
Coll. 16 Oct. 1433 (*Reg. Stafford* (*Bath and Wells*) I 152). D. before 16 Apr. 1435 (*ibid.* II 182).

M. **David Price** D.C.L. (again) 1435–1437.
Coll. 16 Apr. 1435 (*Reg. Stafford* (*Bath and Wells*) II 183). Res. before 9 June 1437 (*ibid.* p. 207).

M. **Peter Stukeley** B.C.L. 1437–1438.
Coll. 9 June 1437 (*Reg. Stafford* (*Bath and Wells*) II 207). Preb. of Wiveliscombe 1438.

William Stephens 1438–1447.
Coll. 12 March 1438 (*Reg. Stafford* (*Bath and Wells*) II 214). D. 27/30 June 1447 (*Som. Med. Wills 1383–1500* pp. 157–9; *Reg. Bekynton* I 79).

M. **Robert Stillington** D.C.L. 1447–1451.
Coll. 30 June 1447 (*Reg. Bekynton* I 79). Adm. 24 July (*ibid.*). Exch. preb. with John Bradston for preb. of Fenton, York, 6 March 1451 (*ibid.* p. 161).

M. **John Bradston** B.Cn.L. 1451–1457.
By exch. March 1451. Adm. 30 March (*Reg. Bekynton* I 161). Res. before 14 June 1457 (*ibid.* p. 286).

M. **John Pope** D.Th. 1457–1476.
Coll. 14 June 1457 (*Reg. Bekynton* I 286). D. 30 Jan./8 Feb. 1476 (PCC 22 Wattys).

M. **John Morton** D.C.L. 1476–1478.
Coll. 9 Feb. 1476 (*Reg. Stillington* p. 107). Bp. of Ely 1478.

M. **Thomas Langton** D.Th., D.Cn.L. 1479–1483.
Coll. 2 Jan. 1479 (*Reg. Stillington* p. 112). Bp. of St Davids 1483.

Henry Edyall 1487–1520.
Adm. 3 Oct. 1487 (*Cal. MSS. D. & C. Wells* II 108). D. by 13 May 1520 (Chichester, Reg. Sherborne I f. 30b; *Cal. MSS. D. & C. Wells* II 204).

M. **John Nase** D.Th. 1530, 1535.
Occ. 1530 (*Reg. Bps., 1518–1559* p. 58). Occ. 1535 (*Valor* I 134). ? Held preb. until d. before 3 March 1538 (*The White Act Book*, ed. W. D. Peckham (Sussex Record Soc., lii) p. 54).

PREBENDARIES OF SHALFORD

Hervey de Staunton 1313–1321.
Mand. adm. 1 Jan. 1313 (*Reg. Drokensford* p. 151). Res. before 11 June 1321 (*ibid.* p. 202).

Robert de Wamberg 1321–1324.
Coll. 11 June 1321 (*Reg. Drokensford* p. 202). Exch. preb. with James de Hispania for preb. of Whitelackington, 26 March 1324 (*ibid.* p. 232).

M. **James de Hispania** 1324–1330.
By exch. March 1324. Exch. preb. with William de Melbourne for preb. of Kinvaston, Wolverhampton royal free chap., Staffs., 30 March 1330 (*Reg. R. de Salopia* I 44).

M. **William de Melbourne** 1330–1331.
By exch. March 1330. Mand. adm. 9 Apr. (*Reg. Baldock, Segrave, Newport et Gravesend*, ed. R. C. Fowler (Canterbury and York Soc., vii) pp. 252–3). Adm. 22 Apr. (*ibid.*). Exch. preb. with Henry de Clyff for ch. of Mold, Flints., 5 Nov. 1331 (*Reg. R. de Salopia* I 76).

M. **Henry de Clyff** 1331–1332.
By exch. Nov. 1331. Exch. preb. with Walter de Burley for preb. of Waltham, Chichester, 14 Sept. 1332 (*Reg. R. de Salopia* I 107).

M. **Walter de Burley** D.Th. 1332–1337.
By exch. Sept. 1332. Res. before 11 March 1337 (*Reg. R. de Salopia* I 330).

M. **Richard de Bynteworth** D.C.L. 1337–1338.
Coll. 11 March 1337 (*Reg. R. de Salopia* I 330). Bp. of London 1338.

M. **Robert de Chykewell** 1339, 1345.
Estate ratif. 20 Aug. 1339 (*CPR. 1338–1340* p. 392). Occ. 12 June 1345 (*CPP.* I 93).

M. **Thomas de Bukton** D.C.L. 1363–1366.
Probably coll. c. Aug. 1363 since mand. adm. unnamed person to preb. 5 Aug. 1363 (*Reg. Sudbury* I 24–5), and royal gr. to Bukton 21 Oct. (*CPR. 1361–1364* p. 405). D. 1366 (*Cal. MSS. D. & C. Wells* II 14).

M. **William de Melbourne** (? again) 1366.
Occ. 16 Oct. 1366 (*Reg. Sudbury* II 171).

Thomas Strete de Knesworth 1366–1368.
Royal gr. 29 Dec. 1366 (*CPR. 1364–1367* p. 347), and 13 July 1367 (*ibid.* p. 424). Exch. preb. with John de Neuport for preb. of Combe Quartadecima, 23 Nov. 1368 (*CPR. 1367–1370* p. 171).

John de Neuport 1368–?
By exch. Nov. 1368. Mand. adm. 3 June and 17 Aug. 1370 (*Reg. Sudbury* I 34–5).

M. **Andrew Baret** D.C.L. ?–1385.
Occ. 22 Feb. 1379 (*Cal. MSS. D. & C. Wells* I 283). Archdcn. of Wells 1385.

John Walrond 1385–1388.
Coll. 31 Oct. 1385 (Lond., Guildhall, Reg. Braybroke f. 41b). Adm. 31 Dec. (*ibid.*). Estate ratif. 28 July 1386 (*CPR. 1385–1389* p. 208). Royal gr. 15 Aug. (*ibid.* p. 207). Exch. preb. with Richard Aldryngton for Epping Upland free chap., Essex, 1 March 1388 (Lond., Guildhall, Reg. Braybroke f. 58b).

Richard Aldryngton 1388–?
Ranulph Hatton 1393.
Aldryngton obtained preb. by exch. March 1388. Estate ratif. 8 Apr. 1390 (*CPR. 1388–1392* p. 235). Royal gr. to Hatton 11 Apr. 1393 (*CPR. 1391–1396* p. 249). Does not appear to have obtained possession since Aldryngton occ. as preb. 27 Aug. 1396 (Lond., Guildhall, Reg. Braybroke f. 145).

Henry Merston ?–1408.

Exch. preb. with William Glym for ch. of Doddington, Cambs. and ch. of Aston Clinton, Bucks., 21/23 Aug. 1408 (*Reg. Bubwith* I 36–7; Ely, Reg. Fordham ff. 106–107).

William Glym 1408–1409.

By exch. Aug. 1408. Adm. 16 Sept. (Lond., Guildhall, Reg. Clifford f. 8b/112b). Exch. preb. with John Wakering for ch. of St Michael, Coventry, 30 July 1409 (*Reg. Bubwith* I 61).

John Wakering 1409–1414.

By exch. July 1409. Exch. preb. with Richard Clifford for preb. of Twiford, St Paul's, London, 28 July 1414 (*Reg. Bubwith* I 179).

Richard Clifford *junior* 1414–1418.

By exch. July 1414. Instal. 6 Aug. (St Paul's MS. WD 13 f. 39b/35b). Res. before 10 Sept. 1418 (*Reg. Bubwith* II 336).

M. Robert Braunche Lic.C.L. 1418–1419.

Coll. 10 Sept. 1418 (*Reg. Bubwith* II 336). Res. 19 Oct. 1419 (*ibid.* p. 376).

John Arundell 1419–1453.

Coll. 20 Oct. 1419 (*Reg. Bubwith* II 376). Res. before 30 Nov. 1453 (*Reg. Bekynton* I 222).

Walter Osborn 1453–1462.

Coll. 30 Nov. 1453 (*Reg. Bekynton* I 222). Adm. 29 Jan. 1454 (Lond., Guildhall, Reg. T. Kempe pt. i f. 29b). Preb. of Combe Octava 1462.

M. John Pemberton 1462–1478.

Coll. 6 Nov. 1462 (*Reg. Bekynton* I 377). Adm. 20 Dec. (Lond., Guildhall, Reg. T. Kempe pt. i f. 84). D. before 15 July 1478 (*Reg. Stillington* p. 111).

M. Thomas Morton 1478–1479.

Coll. 15 July 1478 (*Reg. Stillington* p. 111). Adm. 15 Aug. (Lond., Guildhall, Reg. T. Kempe pt. i f. 168). Preb. of Combe Septima 1479.

Henry Ayra 1479–1480.

Coll. 26 May 1479 (*Reg. Stillington* p. 113). Adm. 5 June (Lond., Guildhall, Reg. T. Kempe pt. i f. 172). D. before 29 March 1480 (*ibid.* f. 181b).

M. William Boket D.Cn.L. 1480–1493.

Adm. 29 Oct. 1480 (Lond., Guildhall, Reg. T. Kempe pt. i f. 181b). Preb. of Whitelackington 1493.

M. Peter Carselegh B.Th. 1493–1536.

Coll. 12 Apr. 1493 (*Reg. Stillington* p. 181). Adm. 30 Apr. (*Cal. MSS. D. & C. Wells* II 128). D. before 24 Jan. 1536 (Lond., Guildhall, Reg. Stokesley ff. 28b–29).

Richard Clarkson 1536–?

Mand. adm. 24 Jan. 1536 (Lond., Guildhall, Reg. Stokesley ff. 28b–29). Adm. 6 Feb. (*ibid.*).

PREBENDARIES OF TAUNTON

John de Kynardeseye 1330–1333.

Coll. 1 Aug. 1330 (*Reg. R. de Salopia* I 58). D. Jan. 1333 (Bodl. Libr., MS. Ashmole 794 f. 72b).

M. **John Logwardyn** D.M. ?–1362.
Occ. 30 Nov. 1360 (*Cal. MSS. D. & C. Wells* I 263). D. before 13 Feb. 1362 (*Reg. R. de Salopia* II 753).

Thomas de Schepton 1362–1381/2.
Coll. 13 Feb. 1362 (*Reg. R. de Salopia* II 753). D. Sept. 1381/2 (*Cal. MSS. D. & C. Wells* II 17).

John Pulteneye ?–1383.
Exch. preb. with James de Billyngsford for ch. of Weston, Suff., 24 March 1383 (Norwich, Reg. Despenser f. 87b).

James de Billyngsford 1383.
By exch. March 1383. Exch. preb. with John de Burton for wardenship of Broseley chap., Salop, 8 May (*Reg. Gilbert* p. 124).

John de Burton 1383–1390.
By exch. May 1383. Estate ratif. 9 May (*CPR. 1385–1389* p. 301). Exch. preb. with Thomas Kyrketon for preb. of Langford Ecclesia, Lincoln, 16 Apr. 1390 (Linc., Reg. XI (Buckingham) f. 433).

M. **Thomas Kyrketon** 1390–?
By exch. Apr. 1390.

Richard Palmer ?–1408.
Res. this preb. before 26 July 1408 (*Reg. Bubwith* I 31).

M. **Henry Gardiner** 1408–1419.
Coll. 26 July 1408 (*Reg. Bubwith* I 31). D. before 26 Nov. 1419 (*ibid.* II 377).

M. **William Lyndwood** D.Cn. & C.L. 1419–1433.
Coll. 26 Nov. 1419 (*Reg. Bubwith* II 377). Res. before 13 Aug. 1433 (*Reg. Stafford (Bath and Wells)* I 145).

Thomas Astel 1433–1439.
Coll. 13 Aug. 1433 (*Reg. Stafford (Bath and Wells)* I 145). D. before 6 June 1439 (*ibid.* II 237).

M. **John Pederton** D.Th. 1439–1460.
Coll. 6 June 1439 (*Reg. Stafford (Bath and Wells)* II 237). D. before 6 June 1460 (*Reg. Bekynton* I 345).

John Roche 1460–1463.
Coll. 6 June 1460 (*Reg. Bekynton* I 345). Preb. of Easton in Gordano 1463.

M. **John Wansford** 1463–1474.
M. **Thomas Purveour** M.A. ?–1469.[1]
M. **Walter Buk** M.A. 1469.
Wansford coll. 2 Jan. 1463 (*Reg. Bekynton* I 380). Buk prov. 5 Oct. 1469 to preb. on d. of Purveour, previous prebendary (*CPL.* XII 350–1). Buk does not appear to have gained possession since Wansford res. preb. Dec. 1474 when preb. of Ashill (*Reg. Stillington* pp. 103, 105).

---

[1] There was probably confusion in the papal chancery between the preb. of Taunton and the preb. of Yatton, since the name is given as 'Thanton', and there is no evidence that Purveour held the preb. of Taunton, but he had been coll. to Yatton in 1451. After Purveour's d. in 1469 there is no record of any coll. to Yatton, and no one occ. as preb. until 1488, and it therefore seems probable that Buk had been prov. to Yatton in 1469, not to Taunton.

F

M. **Richard Fitzjames** M.A. 1475–1497.
Coll. 4 March 1475 (*Reg. Stillington* p. 105). Bp. of Rochester 1497.

M. **Thomas Beaumont** D.Cn. & C.L. 1497–1499.
Adm. 5 Apr. 1497 (*Cal. MSS. D. & C. Wells* II 146). Archdcn. of Bath 1499.

M. **Richard Rawlyns** D.Th. 1499–1500.
Adm. 29 Sept. 1499 (*Cal. MSS. D. & C. Wells* II 156). Res. before 26 Sept. 1500 (*ibid.* p. 159).

M. **Richard Gilberd** 1500–?
Adm. 26 Sept. 1500 (*Cal. MSS. D. & C. Wells* II 159).

M. **William Gilberd** O.Can.S.A., B.Th. Bp. of Maioren.[1] ?–1524/5.
D. as preb. Sept. 1524/5 (*Cal. MSS. D. & C. Wells* II 241).

M. **William Boureman** B.C.L. 1535.
Occ. 1535 (*Valor* I 133).

PREBENDARIES OF TIMBERSCOMBE

Ralph de Knovill ?–1323.
Exch. preb. with Thomas de Hereward for preb. of Credie, Crediton colleg. ch., Devon, 3 Nov. 1323 (Reg. Drokensford f. 203b).

M. **Thomas de Hereward** 1323–1330.
By exch. Nov. 1323. D. before 13 Feb. 1330 (*Reg. R. de Salopia* I 29).

M. **Walter de Burton** D.Th. 1330–?
Coll. 13 Feb. 1330 (*Reg. R. de Salopia* I 29). ? Held preb. until subdean 1334.

M. **John de Carleton** *junior* D.C.L. ?–1365.
Occ. 1 July 1355 (*Reg. R. de Salopia* I 191–2). Exch. preb. and ch. of Sutton-le-Marsh, Lincs., with William Graa of Trusthope for archdcnry of Suffolk, 21 July 1365 (Linc., Reg. x (Buckingham) f. 11b).

William Graa of Trusthope B.Cn. & C.L. 1365–?
By exch. July 1365. Occ. 16 Oct. 1366 (*Reg. Langham* p. 8).

Thomas Horn 1379.
Occ. 22 Feb. 1379 (*Cal. MSS. D. & C. Wells* I 283).

Thomas Hynton 1383.
Occ. 25 Jan. 1383 (*Cal. MSS. D. & C. Wells* I 285).

Thomas Marton 1386–1396.
Royal gr. 9 Aug. 1386 (*CPR. 1385–1389* p. 200). Exch. preb. with Thomas Staundon for preb. of Henbury, Westbury-on-Trym colleg. ch., Glos., 10 Sept. 1396 (Worcester, Reg. Tideman ff. 9b–10).

Thomas Staundon 1396–1407.
By exch. Sept. 1396. Exch. preb. with Hugh Holbache for preb. of Inkberrow, Hereford, 4 May 1407 (*Reg. R. Mascall*, ed. J. H. Parry (Canterbury and York Soc., xxi) p. 183).

M. **Hugh Holbache** D.Cn.L. 1407–?
By exch. May 1407.

John Browning 1419, 1422.
Occ. 29 Apr. 1419 (*Reg. Bubwith* II 356) and 17 Sept. 1422 (*ibid.* p. 422).

[1] He was a suffragan bp. of the abp. of Nazareth.

John Birkhede 1428–1468.
Coll. 11 July 1428 (*Reg. Stafford* (*Bath and Wells*) 1 62). D. 1468 (M. Stephenson, *Monumental Brasses* (1926) p. 302; *Cal. MSS. D. & C. Wells* 11 92).

William Symson 1471.
M. **Robert Wilson** B.Cn. & C.L. 1471–1496.
Wilson adm. 21 Dec. 1471 after certif. issued that John Nesfeld had recovered right of pres. to preb. against William Symson, clerk (*Reg. Stillington* pp. 89–90). D. before 14 Sept. 1496 (*Cal. MSS. D. & C. Wells* 11 145).

M. **Walter Felde** D.Th. 1496–1499.
Adm. 14 Sept. 1496 (*Cal. MSS. D. & C. Wells* 11 145). D. before 15 Apr. 1499 (*Reg. King* p. 29).

M. **John Lugwardyn** 1499–1502.
Coll. 15 Apr. 1499 (*Reg. King* p. 29). Adm. 16 Apr. (*Cal. MSS. D. & C. Wells* 11 155). D. or res. before 17 Sept. 1502 (*ibid.* p. 168).

M. **Thomas Ruthall** D.Cn.L. 1502–1504.
Adm. 18 Sept. 1502 (*Cal. MSS. D. & C. Wells* 11 168). Res. before 22 March 1504 (*CPR. 1494–1509* p. 348).

James Villiers 1504–1511.
Royal gr. 22 March 1504 (*CPR. 1494–1509* p. 348). Adm. 14 May (*Cal. MSS. D. & C. Wells* 11 177). D. before 11 Jan. 1511 (*ibid.* p. 225).

William Villiers 1511–?
Adm. 11 Jan. 1511 (*Cal. MSS. D. & C. Wells* 11 225). Occ. 1535 (*Valor* 1 135).

PREBENDARIES OF WANSTROW

M. **Adam de Orleton** D.Cn.L. 1310–1317.
Mand. adm. after prov. 2 Sept. 1310 (*Reg. Drokensford* p. 31). Bp. of Hereford 1317.

M. **John de Orleton** 1317–?
Gr. lic. 11 Oct. 1317 to execute prov. to preb. (*Cal. MSS. D. & C. Wells* 1 176).

John de Sancto Paulo 1339–?
Royal gr. 3 Aug. 1339 (*CPR. 1338–1340* p. 391). Preb. of Combe Duodecima in 1340, but possibly held Wanstrow until 1349 when abp. of Dublin, since there is no record of any other person holding it until 1352.

M. **John Saucy** B.C.L. 1352.
Estate ratif. 12 Dec. 1352 (*CPR. 1350–1354* p. 374).

M. **Robert de Nettleton** ?–1367.
Occ. 18 Nov. 1366 (*Reg. Langham* p. 68). D. before 14 July 1367 (*CPR. 1364–1367* p. 423).

Richard de Bodenham 1367–?
Royal gr. 14 July 1367 (*CPR. 1364–1367* p. 423).

M. **John Shillyngford** D.C.L. 1379, 1388.
Occ. 12 Feb. 1379 (*Cal. MSS. D. & C. Wells* 1 283). Estate ratif. 20 Apr. 1388 (*CPR. 1385–1389* p. 433). ? Held preb. until d. before Oct. 1406 (Exeter, *Reg. Stafford* 1 f. 308).

M. John Snapp D.Cn.L. ?–1407.
Estate ratif. 14 Oct. 1406 (*CPR. 1405–1408* p. 243). D. before 13 Oct. 1407 (P.R.O., C 47/15/2 (30)).

John Frank 1407–1422.
Coll. 13 Oct. 1407 (P.R.O., C 47/15/2 (30)). Estate ratif. 21 Nov. (*CPR. 1405–1408* p. 369). Royal gr. 23 Dec. (*ibid.* p. 395). Estate ratif. 15 Feb. 1408 (*ibid.* p. 368). Royal mand. adm. 6 Feb. 1409 (*CPR. 1408–1413* p. 48). Res. 19 May, re-adm. 20 May on royal pres.; k. had recovered right of pres. to preb. against bp. Bowet (*Reg. Giffard and Bowet* p. 85). Res. before 27 Aug. 1422 (*Reg. Bubwith* II 421).

Thomas Lane 1422–1424.
Coll. 27 Aug. 1422 (*Reg. Bubwith* II 421). Exch. preb. with John Frank for preb. of Wilmcote, Tamworth colleg. ch., Staffs., 30 Oct. 1424 (*CPR. 1422–1429* p. 233).

John Frank (again) 1424–1427.
By exch. Oct. 1424. Res. before 6 Dec. 1427 (*Reg. Stafford (Bath and Wells)* I 58).

Alan Humberton 1427–1434.
Coll. 6 Dec. 1427 (*Reg. Stafford (Bath and Wells)* I 58). Res. before 19 Feb. 1434 (*ibid.* II 157).

M. John Marchall B.Cn. & C.L. 1434–1446.
Coll. 19 Feb. 1434 (*Reg. Stafford (Bath and Wells)* II 157). Res. before 7 July 1446 (*Reg. Bekynton* I 65).

M. William Crowton M.A. 1446–1477.
Coll. 7 July 1446 (*Reg. Bekynton* I 65). D. 7/31 July 1477 (PCC 30 Wattys).

John Stillington 1477–?
Coll. 20 Oct. 1477 (*Reg. Stillington* p. 110).

M. James Rogers B.C.L. 1501–1545.
Adm. 9 Feb. 1501 (*Cal. MSS. D. & C. Wells* II 161). D. before 1 Nov. 1545 (*Reg. Bps., 1518–1559* p. 113).

PREBENDARIES OF WARMINSTER AL. LUXVILLE

M. John de Lacy 1299–1301.
Coll. 11 June 1299 (*Reg. Gandavo* II 597). Adm. 18 June (*Cal. MSS. D. & C. Wells* I 159). D. before 23 Dec. 1301 (*Reg. Gandavo* II 609).

M. James de Berkeley D.Th. 1302–1326.
Coll. 10 Jan. 1302 (*Reg. Gandavo* II 609). Bp. of Exeter 1326.

M. Adam de Burley M.A. 1327–1328.
Prov. 1 May 1327 (*CPL.* II 258). D. before Aug. 1328 (*Reg. Drokensford* p. 292).

M. John de Sydenhale M.A. 1341–1353.
Adm. 12 Sept. 1341 (Salis., Reg. Wyville II ii f. 95b). Exch. preb. with William de Salton for preb. of Easton in Gordano, 4 Sept. 1353 (*Reg. R. de Salopia* II 724).

M. William de Salton 1353–1354.
By exch. Sept. 1353. D. before 16 March 1354 (*Reg. R. de Salopia* II 724).

John de Blebury 1354–1363.
Royal gr. 16 March 1354 (*Reg. R. de Salopia* II 724). Preb. of Litton 1363.

William de Wykeham ?–1363.

Exch. preb. with William de Bokbridge for preb. of Crowhurst, Hastings royal free chap., Suss., 19 Feb. 1363 (*Reg. R. de Salopia* II 758).

William de Bokbridge 1363–1366.

By exch. Feb. 1363. Exch. preb. with John de Buttele for free chap. of St Margaret, Chelmsford, Essex, 15 Oct. 1366 (*Reg. Sudbury* I 252).

John de Buttele 1366–?
By exch. Oct. 1366.[1]

Thomas Salter ?–1379.

Occ. 12 Feb. 1379 (*Cal. MSS. D. & C. Wells* I 282). D. before 26 Sept. (Salis., Reg. Erghum ff. 30b–31).

M. **Walter Wyncaulton** 1379–1410.

Coll. 26 Sept. 1379 (Salis., Reg. Erghum ff. 30b–31). Mand. adm. 2 Oct. (*ibid.*). D. before 13 Jan. 1410 (*Reg. Bubwith* I 2).

Thomas Shelford 1410.

Coll. 13 Jan. 1410 (*Reg. Bubwith* I 2). Preb. of Dultingcote in Apr.

Richard Gabriell 1410.

Coll. 17 Apr. 1410 (*Reg. Bubwith* I 8). Exch. preb. with John Morehay for ch. of Ipplepen, Devon, 30 May (*ibid.* p. 9).

John Morehay 1410–1411.

By exch. May 1410. Res. 28 Feb. 1411 (*Reg. Bubwith* I 21–2).

John Dyppull *or* **Brymesgrave** 1411–?

Coll. 28 Feb. 1411 (*Reg. Bubwith* I 22). Adm. 20 March (Salis., Reg. Hallum f. 23).

M. **John Urry** 1429–1434.

Coll. 25 Oct. 1429 (*Reg. Stafford (Bath and Wells)* I 74). D. before 7 June 1434 (*ibid.* II 163).

M. **Henry Penwortham** 1434–1438/9.

Coll. 7 June 1434 (*Reg. Stafford (Bath and Wells)* II 163). D. 27 Sept. 1438/9 (*Reg. of H. Chichele*, ed. E. F. Jacob (Canterbury and York Soc., xlii, xlv–xlvii) II 574–6; *Cal. MSS. D. & C. Wells* II 70).

John Chichele 1457/8.
Occ. 1457/8 (*Cal. MSS. D. & C. Wells* II 89).

John Howell ?–1478.
Res. this preb. before 2 June 1478 (*Reg. Stillington* p. 111).

M. **William Godde** B.Cn.L. 1478–?
Coll. 2 June 1478 (*Reg. Stillington* p. 111).

William Stillington ?–1500.
Res. this preb. before 8 March 1500 (*Reg. King* p. 47).

M. **William Soper** M.A. 1500–1519.

Coll. 8 March 1500 (*Reg. King* p. 47). Adm. 12 March (*Cal. MSS. D. & C. Wells* II 157). ? Held preb. until d. before May 1519 (*Emden, Reg. Ox.* III 1729).

[1] John de Crykkelade occ. as preb. of 'Luxton' 17 Oct. 1366 (*Reg. Sudbury* II 176–7). This must be an error for Litton rather than Luxville, since negotiations for his obtaining the preb. of Litton must have been in process by 17 Oct. He obtained it 28 Oct. 1366.

M. Roger Eggeworth D.Th. 1535.

Occ. 1535 (*Valor* I 134). ? Held preb. until 1554 when chancellor (*Reg. Bps.*, *1518–1559* pp. 120–1).

PREBENDARIES OF WEDMORE PRIMA

This prebend was attached to the deanery.

PREBENDARIES OF WEDMORE SECUNDA

M. Thomas de Cobham D.Cn.L. 1299–1317.

Adm. 13 Dec. 1299 (*Cal. MSS. D. & C. Wells* I 159). Bp. of Worcester 1317.

M. Lawrence de la Barre 1317–1336.

Prov. 18 May 1317 (*CPL.* II 151). D. before 11 Oct. 1336 (*Reg. R. de Salopia* I 276).

Robert de Sambourne 1366.

Occ. 18 Nov. 1366 (*Reg. Langham* p. 68).

Roger Wyte ?–1372/3.

D. as preb. Sept. 1372/3 (*Cal. MSS. D. & C. Wells* II 13).

John Colyngtree 1379.

Occ. 22 Feb. and 4 March 1379 (*Cal. MSS. D. & C. Wells* I 283, 284).

Ralph Berners ?–1397/8.

D. as preb. Sept. 1397/8 (*Cal. MSS. D. & C. Wells* II 31).

M. Gilbert Stone ?–1401.

Occ. 21 Jan. 1400 (*CPL.* V 315). Exch. preb. with John Gamull for preb. of Eigne, Hereford, and preb. of Wilmcote, Tamworth colleg. ch., Staffs., 5 March 1401 (*CPR. 1399–1401* pp. 442–3.)

John Gamull 1401–1408.

By exch. March 1401. Royal gr. 24 March and 11 Apr. (*CPR. 1399–1401* pp. 468, 473). D. before 17 Feb. 1408 (*Reg. Giffard and Bowet* p. 73).

Thomas Shelford 1408–1410.

Coll. 17 Feb. 1408 (*Reg. Giffard and Bowet* p. 73). Preb. of Warminster al. Luxville 1410.

Henry Mory 1410–1423.

Coll. 13 Jan. 1410 (*Reg. Bubwith* I 2). Exch. preb. with John Elys for ch. of Christian Malford, Wilts., 24 Jan. 1423 (*ibid.* II 428).

John Elys 1423.

By exch. Jan. 1423. Res. before 11 June (*Reg. Bubwith* II 435).

M. William Felter D.Cn.L. 1423–?

Coll. 11 June 1423 (*Reg. Bubwith* II 435). Probably res. in Oct. when preb. of Whitelackington.

M. Adam Moleyns D.C.L. 1436–1441.

Coll. 1 March 1436 (*Reg. Stafford* (*Bath and Wells*) II 193). Archdcn. of Taunton 1441.

M. John Delaberd B.Cn.L. 1441–1447.

Coll. 5 Jan. 1441 (*Reg. Stafford* (*Bath and Wells*) II 261). Bp. of St Davids 1447.

John Trevenaunt 1447–1450.
Coll. 20 Dec. 1447 (*Reg. Bekynton* I 85). Preb. of Combe Duodecima and provost 1450.

Thomas Kirkeby 1450–1459.
Coll. 5 Apr. 1450 (*Reg. Bekynton* I 144). D. before 3 Apr. 1459 (*ibid*. p. 316).

M. Henry Webber B.Cn.L. 1459–1477.
Coll. 3 Apr. 1459 (*Reg. Bekynton* I 316). D. before 1 March 1477 (*Reg. T. Bourg-chier*, ed. F. R. H. Du Boulay (Canterbury and York Soc., liv) p. 214).

M. Peter Huse B.Cn.L. 1477–1494.
Coll. 16 July 1477 (*Reg. Stillington* p. 110). Res. before 12 Feb. 1494 (*ibid*. p. 189).

M. Andrew Bensted M.A. 1494–1505.
Coll. 12 Feb. 1494 (*Reg. Stillington* p. 189). Adm. 9 March (*Cal. MSS. D. & C. Wells* II 135). Res. before 22 July 1505 (*ibid*. p. 182).

M. John Edmondys B.Cn. & C.L. 1505–1520.
Adm. 22 July 1505 (*Cal. MSS. D. & C. Wells* II 182). D. before 29 Sept. 1520 (*ibid*. p. 240).

M. William Wyneyarde M.A. ?–1541.
Occ. 1535 (*Valor* I 134). D. May/23 June 1541 (Lamb., Reg. Cranmer f. 264; *Reg. Bps.*, *1518–1559* p. 90).

M. Robert Talbot 1541–?
Coll. 23 June 1541 (*Reg. Bps.*, *1518–1559* p. 90).

PREBENDARIES OF WEDMORE TERCIA

Robert de Sambourne ?–1382.
Occ. 12 Feb. 1379 (*Cal. MSS. D. & C. Wells* I 282). D. 20 May/12 Sept. 1382 (*Som. Med. Wills* *1501–1530* pp. 287–8).

M. Thomas Frome B.C.L. 1401.
Estate ratif. 13 Apr. 1401 (*CPR. 1401–1405* p. 9).

Alexander Hody[1] ?–1420.
Exch. preb. with John Cole for preb. in St Crantock's colleg. ch., Cornw., 17 Dec. 1420 (*Reg. Bubwith* II 397–8).

John Cole 1420–1433/4.
By exch. Dec. 1420. Adm. 20 Dec. (*Reg. Bubwith* II 397–8). D. Sept. 1433/4 (*Cal. MSS. D. & C. Wells* II 68).

Thomas Assheden 1441–1450.
Coll. 13 Apr. 1441 (*Reg. Stafford* (*Bath and Wells*) II 270). D. before 19 Oct. 1450 (*Reg. Bekynton* I 155).

M. Oliver Dynham M.A. 1450–1454.
Coll. 19 Oct. 1450 (*Reg. Bekynton* I 155). Preb. of Buckland Dinham 1454.

M. Hugh Sugar *or* Norris D.C.L. 1454–1460.
Coll. 17 Sept. 1454 (*Reg. Bekynton* I 237). Preb. of Combe Septima 1460.

M. William King B.A. 1460–1463.
Coll. 4 May 1460 (*Reg. Bekynton* I 344). Preb. of Combe Decima 1463.

[1] Hody was probably coll. to this preb. in 1419 when he res. preb. of Wedmore Quarta.

John Pedewell 1464–?
Coll. 1 Jan. 1464 (*Reg. Bekynton* I 407).

M. Nicholas Halswell D.M. 1492–1505.
Adm. 30 June 1492 (*Cal. MSS. D. & C. Wells* II 126). Res. before 25 Apr. 1505 (*ibid.* p. 181).

M. John Taylour D.Cn.L. 1505–?
Adm. 25 Apr. 1505 by proxy (*Cal. MSS. D. & C. Wells* II 181), in person 13 Nov. 1506 (*ibid.* p. 198). ? Held preb. until 1522 when preb. of Yatton.

M. Walter Cretynge D.C.L. ?–1557.
Occ. 1535 (*Valor* I 134). D. 2/20 Nov. 1557 (PCC 49 Wrastley; *Reg. Bps., 1518–1559* p. 149).

PREBENDARIES OF WEDMORE QUARTA

Ralph de Windelzore 1313–1351.
Adm. 30 June 1313 (*Cal. MSS. D. & C. Wells* I 155). Exch. preb. with Richard de Likamstede for preb. and canonry in St Mary's colleg. ch., Warwick, 16 Jan. 1351 (*Reg. R. de Salopia* II 685).

Richard de Likamstede 1351–?
By exch. Jan. 1351.

Robert atte Sloo 1361.
Occ. 6 Oct. 1361 (*Cal. MSS. D. & C. Wells* I 264).

William de Odecumbe 1362–?
Coll. 22 Apr. 1362 (*Reg. R. de Salopia* II 762). Occ. as preb. of Combe Septima 1366.

William Cockham 1373, 1379.
Estate ratif. 22 March 1373 (*CPR. 1370–1374* p. 262). Occ. 12 Feb. 1379 (*Cal. MSS. D. & C. Wells* I 282).

John Bonyngton ?–1409.
D. as preb. before 13 Apr. 1409 (*Reg. Bubwith* I 52).

John Roland 1409.
Coll. 13 Apr. 1409 (*Reg. Bubwith* I 52). Preb. of Combe Tercia in Dec.

M. Henry Abendon D.Th. 1410.
Coll. 12 Jan. 1410 (*Reg. Bubwith* I 70). Preb. of Wedmore Quinta 20 Jan.

M. Thomas Frome B.C.L. ?–1418.
Res. this preb. for preb. of Combe Quinta 1418 (*Reg. Bubwith* I 298, 306).

Alexander Hody 1418–1419.
Coll. 26 Jan. 1418 (*Reg. Bubwith* I 306). Res. before 25 Oct. 1419 (*ibid.* II 376).[1]

M. Nicholas Steur M.A. 1419–1422.
Coll. 25 Oct. 1419 (*Reg. Bubwith* II 376). D. before 13 July 1422 (*ibid.* p. 420).

John Depeden 1422–1424.
Coll. 13 July 1422 (*Reg. Bubwith* II 420). Res. before 7 Apr. 1424 (*ibid.* p. 450).

M. William Brett 1424–?
Coll. 7 Apr. 1424 (*Reg. Bubwith* II 450).

[1] Hody was probably coll. to the preb. of Wedmore Tercia in this year—1419.

John Depeden (again) 1437.
Occ. 9 Feb. 1437 (*CPL.* VIII 577).

M. Robert Aiscough M.A. 1439–1448.
Coll. 12 Feb. 1439 (*Reg. Stafford* (*Bath and Wells*) II 234). Res. before 18 May 1448 (*Reg. Bekynton* I 95).

M. Nicholas Cloos D.Th. 1448–1450.
Coll. 14 May 1448 (*Reg. Bekynton* I 95). Bp. of Carlisle 1450.

M. John Kyrkeby M.A. 1450–1451.
Coll. 5 Apr. 1450 (*Reg. Bekynton* I 144). Preb. of Wiveliscombe 1451.

John Bochell 1451–1453.
Coll. 2 July 1451 (*Reg. Bekynton* I 165). D. before 30 May 1453 (*ibid.* p. 206).

M. Thomas Merssh B.Cn. & C.L. 1453–1457.
Coll. 30 May 1453 (*Reg. Bekynton* I 206). Preb. of Henstridge 1457.

M. Richard Swan M.A. 1457–1459.
Coll. 14 June 1457 (*Reg. Bekynton* I 286). Preb. of Combe Duodecima 1459.

M. Robert Peuesy B.Cn. & C.L. 1459–1464.
Coll. 23 June 1459 (*Reg. Bekynton* I 323). D. before 19 Apr. 1464 (*ibid.* p. 413).

M. John Baker D.Th. 1464–1488.
Coll. 19 Apr. 1464 (*Reg. Bekynton* I 413). D. before 27 Feb. 1488 (*Cal. MSS. D. & C. Wells* II 110).

William Burton 1488–?
Adm. 27 Feb. 1488 (*Cal. MSS. D. & C. Wells* II 110).

M. William Horsey D.Cn.L. 1511–1543.
Adm. 5 June 1511 (*Cal. MSS. D. & C. Wells* II 226). D. before 13 Apr. 1543 (*Reg. Bps., 1518–1559* p. 101).

PREBENDARIES OF WEDMORE QUINTA

William de Cammel[1] ?–1361.
Occ. 10 June 1352, was then said to have held preb. for two years and more (*CPP.* I 228). Preb. of Combe Quinta 1361.

John de Pulle 1361–?
Mand. adm. 1 Sept. 1361 (*Cal. MSS. D. & C. Wells* I 263).

Roger de Wytehurst 1366.
Occ. 1366 (*Reg. Langham* p. 68).

John Balton 1379.
Occ. 12 Feb. 1379 (*Cal. MSS. D. & C. Wells* I 282).

M. John de Upton 1390.
Estate ratif. 23 May 1390 (*CPR. 1388–1392* p. 249). D. 5 Sept. 1396/22 Jan. 1397, not called preb. (Lamb., Reg. Arundell I ff. 153–155).

M. Henry Abendon D.Th. 1410–?
Coll. 20 Jan. 1410 (*Reg. Bubwith* I 2). ? Res. 1419 when preb. of Combe Undecima, but since no coll. to Wedmore Quinta is mentioned in 1419, he possibly held preb. until 1427.

[1] Walter le Wyte possibly held this preb. before Cammel. There is a mand. adm. Cammel to preb. held by Wyte, 31 Jan. 1348 (*Reg. R. de Salopia* II 577).

Thomas Humphrey *or* **Umfray** 1427–1433.
Coll. 9 Nov. 1427 (*Reg. Stafford (Bath and Wells)* I 57). Res. before 16 Apr. 1433 (*ibid.* p. 141).

Walter Shiryngton 1433–1449.
Coll. 16 Apr. 1433 (*Reg. Stafford (Bath and Wells)* I 141). D. before 21 Feb. 1449 (*Reg. Bekynton* I 109).

Richard Hayman 1449–1452.
Coll. 21 Feb. 1449 (*Reg. Bekynton* I 109). Preb. of Litton 1452.

M. **John Pope** D.Th. 1452–1453.
Coll. 12 Apr. 1452 (*Reg. Bekynton* I 179). Preb. of Combe Tercia 1453.

Thomas Downe 1453–?
Coll. 6 Apr. 1453 (*Reg. Bekynton* I 203).[1]

M. **William Slaughter** B.Cn.L. ?–1494.
D. as preb. 22 Oct./15 Nov. 1494 (PCC 17 Vox).

M. **Richard Hatton** D.C.L. 1495–1509.
Royal gr. 9 Feb. 1495 (*CPR. 1494-1509* p. 13). Adm. 9 Apr. (*Cal. MSS. D. & C. Wells* II 140). D. before 29 May 1509 (*ibid.* p. 213).

M. **William Haryngton** D.C.L. 1509–1523.
Adm. by proxy 29 May 1509 (*Cal. MSS. D. & C. Wells* II 213), in person 13 Sept. (*ibid.* p. 215). D. before 25 Nov. 1523 (Lond., Guildhall, Reg. Tunstal f. 5; *Cal. MSS. D. & C. Wells* II 241.)

Robert Blasgrove 1535.
Occ. 1535 (*Valor* I 136).

PREBENDARIES OF WHITCHURCH

John de Grandisson ?–1327.
Occ. 10 July 1320 (*Cal. MSS. D. & C. Wells* I 191). Bp. of Exeter 1327.

M. **William de Grandisson** 1327–1330.
Prov. 14 Dec. 1327 (*CPL.* II 265). D. 5 June 1330 (Exeter, Reg. Grandisson III f. 14).

M. **Thomas de Garton** 1330.
Occ. 1330 (*Reg. R. de Salopia* I 61).

Robert de Luffenham ?–1348.
D. as preb. c. 1348 (*CPL.* III 537).

M. **Richard de Tormeton** B.Cn. & C.L. 1348–?
Coll. c. 1348, since in Oct. 1354 said to have held preb. for six years (*CPP.* I 263). Estate ratif. 13 July 1350 (*CPR. 1348-1350* p. 548). Papal conf. 16 Nov. 1354 (*CPL.* III 537). ? Held preb. until d. before 4 July 1361 (*CPP.* I 370).

Thomas Edington ?–1366.
Res. this preb. before 17 Oct. 1366 (*Reg. Langham* p. 28; *Cal. MSS. D. & C. Wells* I 269).

Robert Remston of Corffe 1366–?
Occ. 17 Oct. 1366 (*Reg. Langham* p. 28). Adm. 18 Oct. (*Cal. MSS. D. & C. Wells* I 269). Royal gr. 12 May 1367 (*CPR. 1364-1367* p. 393).

---

[1] Henry Sharp who res. a preb. of Wedmore in 1472 and William Chokke who was coll. to succeed him possibly were prebs. of Wedmore Quinta (*Reg. Stillington* pp. 94–5).

Nicholas Ford ?–1374.
Occ. as 'late' preb. of Whitchurch 30 Sept. 1374 (P.R.O., C 85/38/27).

M. Richard Courtenay B.C.L. ?–1410.
Occ. 16 June 1408 (*Reg. Giffard and Bowet* p. 75). Estate ratif. 27 Feb. 1410 (*CPR. 1408–1413* p. 117). Dean in May.

M. William Spaldyngton B.Cn.L. 1410.
Coll. 29 June 1410 (*Reg. Bubwith* I 10). Res. before 9 Nov. (*ibid.* p. 13).

M. John Stokes Lic.C.L. 1410.
Coll. 9 Nov. 1410 (*Reg. Bubwith* I 13). Exch. preb. with Robert Keten for ch. of Corhampton, Hants, s.d. (*ibid.*).

M. Robert Keten Lic.Cn. & C.L. 1410–1429.
By exch. Nov. 1410. D. 11/25 Aug. 1429 (PCC 12 Luffenam).

M. John Daventry D.Th. 1429–1439.
Coll. 26 Aug. 1429 (*Reg. Stafford (Bath and Wells)* I 72). D. 19/28 Apr. 1439 (PCC 25 Luffenam).

John Lane ?–1447.
Occ. 3 Apr. 1442 (*Reg. Stafford (Bath and Wells)* II 276–7). D. before 6 June 1447 (*Reg. Bekynton* I 77).

M. Robert Stillington D.C.L. 1447.
Coll. 6 June 1447 (*Reg. Bekynton* I 77). Preb. of St Decumans 30 June.

M. John Morton D.Th. 1447–1463.
Coll. 25 July 1447 (*Reg. Bekynton* I 79). D. before 30 Dec. 1463 (*ibid.* p. 407).

M. Thomas Chaundeler D.Th. 1463–1490.
Coll. 30 Dec. 1463 (*Reg. Bekynton* I 407). Occ. 23 Apr. 1487 (*Reg. Stillington* p. 142). Res. before 20 May 1490 (*Cal. MSS. D. & C. Wells* II 119).[1]

M. Robert Sherburn B.M. 1490–1493.
Adm. 20 May 1490 (*Cal. MSS. D. & C. Wells* II 119). Res. before 2 Nov. 1493 (*Reg. Stillington* p. 187).

M. John Hill 1493–?[2]
Coll. 2 Nov. 1493 (*Reg. Stillington* p. 187). Adm. 14 Nov. (*Cal. MSS. D. & C. Wells* II 135).

Thomas Clifford 1500–1509.
Adm. 4 Dec. 1500 (*Cal. MSS. D. & C. Wells* II 160). D. before 1 Dec. 1509 (*ibid.* p. 219).

M. John Claymonde M.A. 1509–1537.
Adm. by proxy 1 Dec. 1509 (*Cal. MSS. D. & C. Wells* II 219), in person 11 Sept. 1510 (*ibid.* p. 223). D. 19 Nov. 1537 (*Emden, Reg. Ox.* I 428).

John Fitzjames 1541.
Occ. 5 March 1541 (*Cal. MSS. D. & C. Wells* II 253).

[1] Chaundeler d. by 2 Nov. 1490 (*Reg. T. Myllyng*, ed. A. T. Bannister (Canterbury and York Soc., xxvi) p. 198).
[2] Hill possibly res. this preb. soon after his coll. since he d. as preb. of Barton St David before 1 Feb. 1494, but might have held both prebs. *in commendam* or by dispensation.

PREBENDARIES OF WHITELACKINGTON

M. James de Hispania ?–1324.
Exch. preb. with Robert de Wamberg for preb. of Shalford, 26 March 1324 (*Reg. Drokensford* p. 232).

Robert de Wamberg 1324–1326.
By exch. March 1324. Exch. preb. and ch. of Market Lavington, Wilts., with Wibert de Lutleton for archdcnry of Wells, 13 June 1326 (Reg. Drokensford f. 25).

M. Wibert de Lutleton B.C.L. 1326–?
Thomas de Hakelut 1337, 1366.
Richard de Chippenham 1337.
Lutleton obtained preb. by exch. June 1326. Hakelut prov. to preb. in Wells 27 Feb. 1330 (*CPL.* II 307). Estate of Lutleton as preb. of Whitelackington ratif. 10 Feb. 1331 (*CPR. 1330–1334* p. 77) and occ. as preb. 1 June 1332 (*Reg. R. de Salopia* I 94). Bp. cited 25 Aug. 1337 to appear in abp's court because Chippenham had been intruded into preb. of Whitelackington and was disturbing possession of Hakelut (*ibid.* p. 309). Hakelut retained possession, occ. as preb. 18 Nov. 1366 (*Reg. Langham* p. 39). ? Held preb. until d. 1375 (*Reg. Gilbert* p. 107).

M. Thomas Byngham M.Th. 1390.
Estate ratif. 14 July 1390 (*CPR. 1388–1392* p. 298).

M. Richard Drayton B.Cn.L. ?–1415.
Occ. 20 Apr. 1414 (*Cal. MSS. D. & C. Wells* I 445). D. before 9 March 1415 (*Reg. Bubwith* I 203).

Simon Gaunstede 1415–1423.
Coll. 9 March 1415 (*Reg. Bubwith* I 203). D. before 11 Oct. 1423 (*ibid.* II 445).

M. William Felter D.Cn.L. 1423–1435.
Coll. 11 Oct. 1423 (*Reg. Bubwith* II 445). Res. before 23 June 1435 (*Reg. Stafford* (*Bath and Wells*) II 184).

John Bate 1435–1442.
Coll. 23 June 1435 (*Reg. Stafford* (*Bath and Wells*) II 184). Res. before 21 June 1442 (*ibid.* p. 278).

John Winsford 1442–?
Coll. 21 June 1442 (*Reg. Stafford* (*Bath and Wells*) II 278).

M. Thomas Bromehale B.Cn. & C.L. 1463–1479.
Coll. 2 Jan. 1463 (*Reg. Bekynton* I 380). D. before 14 May 1479 (*Reg. Stillington* p. 113).

John Lascy 1479–1493.
Coll. 14 May 1479 (*Reg. Stillington* p. 113). D. before 16 Apr. 1493 (*ibid.* p. 181).

M. William Boket D.Cn.L. 1493–1500.
Coll. 16 Apr. 1493 (*Reg. Stillington* p. 181). D. before 25 May 1500 (*Reg. King* p. 49).

M. John Hogekyn D.Th. 1500–1505.
Adm. 3 Aug. 1500 (*Cal. MSS. D. & C. Wells* II 159). Res. before 20 Oct. 1505 (*ibid.* p. 184).

Richard Philpot 1505–?

Adm. 20 Oct. 1505 by proxy (*Cal. MSS. D. & C. Wells* II 184), in person 6 Jan. 1507 (*ibid.* p. 200).

M. James Fitzjames D.Th. ?–1524.

Res. this preb. before 14 Nov. 1524 when preb. of Wormenstre (*Reg. Bps.*, *1518–1559* p. 37).

M. Edmund Wylde 1524–1546.

Coll. 15 Nov. 1524 (*Reg. Bps.*, *1518–1559* p. 37). D. before 23 Feb. 1546 (*ibid.* p. 113).

PREBENDARIES OF WIVELISCOMBE

Robert de Haselscawe 1310, 1321.

John de Sandale 1310–?

Haselscawe held preb. while provost (*Cal. MSS. D. & C. Wells* I 250). Occ. as provost 7 Aug. 1310 (Reg. Drokensford f. 52). Royal gr. to Sandale 11 Sept. (*CPR. 1307–1313* p. 277). Royal prohibn. 23 Oct. against persons disturbing peaceful possession of preb. and provostship (*ibid.* p. 285). Haselscawe appears to have retained possession, occ. 24 Feb. 1321 (*Reg. Drokensford* p. 200).

Robert de Hillum 1330.

Gerard de Sudbury ?–1332.

Hillum occ. as preb. 16 Sept. 1330 (*CPR. 1330–1334* p. 6). Estate ratif. 31 Oct. (*ibid.* p. 14). Sudbury claimed preb. by virtue of prov. but unable to obtain possession, appeal to curia by both parties, Sudbury judged to be lawful claimant, but d. before 6 July 1332 without gaining possession (*CPL.* II 374).

Robert de Taunton 1332–?

Isuard Gascy O.S.B. 1332–1346.

Reginald de Donyngton 1343.

William de Kyldesby 1345.

Royal gr. to Taunton 16 June 1332 (*Reg. R. de Salopia* I 159). Gascy prov. 6 July (*CPL.* II 374). Royal prohibn. 21 Apr. 1334 against ecclesiastical persons proceeding against k's right to pres. to preb. (*CPR. 1330–1334* p. 539). Taunton d. n.d. while suit still pending (*Cal. MSS. D. & C. Wells* I 250). Mand. adm. Gascy 4 June (*Reg. R. de Salopia* I 169). Royal gr. to Donyngton 24 Aug. 1343 (*CPR. 1343–1345* p. 120). Royal gr. to Kyldesby 28 Apr. 1345 (*ibid.* p. 466). Gascy appears to have retained possession since exch. preb. with John de Derby for priorate of secular ch. of St Leger, Laupjubeo, St Genis, canton of Serres, dioc. Gap, France, 18 Sept. 1346 (*CPL.* III 217; *CPP.* I 118).

John de Derby 1346–1347.

By exch. Sept. 1346. Exch. preb. with John de Offord for preb. of Combe Undecima, 21 Feb. 1347 (*Reg. R. de Salopia* II 540).

M. John de Offord D.C.L. 1347–1348.

By exch. Feb. 1347. Abp. of Canterbury 1348.

M. William de Bergevenny D.Th. 1348.

Preb. reserved for Bergevenny 28 Jan. 1348 (*CPL.* III 273).

Robert Carswell ?–1375.

Occ. 19 July 1364 (*Reg. L. de Charltone*, ed. J. H. Parry (Canterbury and York Soc., xiv) p. 71). D. before 1 Oct. 1375 (*Cal. MSS. D. & C. Wells* I 274, 278).

M. Thomas Spert D.C.L. 1376-1397/8.

Royal gr. 27 May 1376 (*CPR. 1374-1377* p. 273). Royal mand. 6 Nov. to arrest all persons proceeding against k's coll. of Spert to preb. (*ibid.* p. 413). Occ. as can. of Wells 1377 (P.R.O., E 179/4/1). Chancellor 1382 but retained preb., d. Sept. 1397/8 Jan. 1398 (*Cal. MSS. D. & C. Wells* II 33; Salis., Reg. Medford f. 59).

M. Richard Clifford *senior* 1398-1400.

Royal gr. 27 Jan. 1398 (*CPR. 1396-1399* p. 278). Estate ratif. 14 Oct. 1399 (*CPR. 1399-1401* p. 3). Bp. of Bath and Wells 1400.

Angelo Acciaioli Card. bp. of Ostia. 1400.

M. John Bathe M.A. 1400-1438.

Preb. reserved for Acciaioli 12 May 1400 (*CPL.* v 289-90). Royal gr. to Bathe 27 July (*CPR. 1399-1401* p. 351), and 15 Sept. 1401 (*ibid.* p. 539). Coll. by bp. 2 Nov. (*Reg. Giffard and Bowet* p. 19). Estate ratif. 20 Dec. 1402 (*CPR. 1401-1405* p. 158). D. before 10 March 1438 (*Reg. Stafford (Bath and Wells)* II 214).

M. Peter Stukeley B.C.L. 1438-1451.

Coll. 10 March 1438 (*Reg. Stafford (Bath and Wells)* II 214). D. before 3 May 1451 (*Reg. Bekynton* I 163).

M. John Kyrkeby M.A. 1451-1459.

Coll. 12 May 1451 (*Reg. Bekynton* I 162-3). D. before 26 June 1459 (*ibid.* p. 323).

M. Richard Worthington B.Cn.L. 1459-1487.

Coll. 26 June 1459 (*Reg. Bekynton* I 323). Preb. of Combe Duodecima and provost 1487.

M. Edward Willughby M.A. 1497-1509.

Adm. 6 Oct. 1497 (*Cal. MSS. D. & C. Wells* II 108). D. before 29 Apr. 1509 (*ibid.* p. 213).

M. John Chamber D.M. 1509-?

Adm. 29 Apr. 1509 (*Cal. MSS. D. & C. Wells* II 213). Occ. 1535 (*Valor* I 134). ? Held preb. until d. 1549 (*Emden, Reg. Ox.* I 385).

PREBENDARIES OF WORMENSTRE

Thomas de Haselschawe 1343.

Thomas de Hatfield 1343-1345.

Haselschawe occ. as preb. 12 Feb. 1343 (*Reg. R. de Salopia* II 460). Royal gr. to Hatfield 10 May (*CPR. 1343-1345* p. 16). Proctors appointed 5 July to prosecute appeal about the preb. which Haselschawe claiming unlawfully (*Reg. R. de Salopia* II 465). Preb. sequestered by bp. 13 July 1344 (*ibid.* p. 411). Hatfield bp. of Durham 1345.

John de Wynwyk 1347-?

Royal gr. 8 Nov. 1347 (*CPR. 1345-1348* p. 428). Mand. from k. 11 Feb. 1348 to arrest all persons appealing against judgt. by which k. had recovered right to pres. to preb. (*CPR. 1348-1350* p. 66). Estate of Wynwyk ratif. 20 Nov. 1351 (*CPR. 1350-1354* p. 179) and 20 Sept. 1352 (*ibid.* p. 324).

Richard de Rodeneye ?-1361.

D. as preb. before 23 Aug. 1361 (*Cal. MSS. D. & C. Wells* I 263).

M. Edmund Gournay Sch.C.L. 1361-?

Mand. adm. 23 Aug. 1361 (*Cal. MSS. D. & C. Wells* I 263).

William de Cammel 1366.
Occ. 18 Nov. 1366 (*Reg. Langham* p. 68).

John Dele 1368–?
Royal gr. 22 May 1368 (*CPR. 1367–1370* p. 116).

Thomas Lynton 1386–?
Royal gr. 2 Aug. 1386 (*CPR. 1385–1389* p. 197).

M. William Lambrok ?–1439.
Raynald de Brancacio Card. dcn. of SS. Vitus et Modestus. ?–1393.
M. Andrew Baret D.C.L. ?–1393.
Raynald de Brancacio claimed preb. by virtue of prov. but unable to obtain possession since occupied by Lambrok (*CPL.* IV 468–9). Royal mand. 1 Dec. 1391 citing persons disturbing possession of Lambrok (*CPR. 1391–1396* p. 77). Appeal by both parties to curia, sentence given in favour of Raynald de Brancacio and perpetual silence imposed upon Lambrok, but refused to resign. Sentence of excomm. imposed upon him by pope Urban VI, but reinstated by pope Boniface IX 5 July 1393 (*CPL.* IV 468–9). Baret res. claim to preb. s.d., had claimed preb. by virtue of prov. (*ibid.*). Estate of Lambrok ratif. 12 Nov. 1399 (*CPR. 1399–1401* p. 56). D. before 21 Apr. 1439 (*Reg. Stafford (Bath and Wells)* II 236).

M. Thomas Bekynton D.C.L. 1439–1441.
Coll. 21 Apr. 1439 (*Reg. Stafford (Bath and Wells)* II 236). Preb. of Dultingcote 1441.

Richard Corff 1441–1444.
Coll. 11 Apr. 1441 (*Reg. Stafford (Bath and Wells)* II 269). D. before 29 Jan. 1444 (*Reg. Bekynton* I 6).

M. John Bernard B.Cn.L. 1444–1460.
Coll. 29 Jan. 1444 (*Reg. Bekynton* I 6). Mand. adm. 31 Jan. (*ibid.* p. 7). D. before 30 Apr. 1460 (*ibid.* p. 343).

M. Thomas Austell B.Cn.L. 1460–1515.
Coll. 30 Apr. 1460 (*Reg. Bekynton* I 363). D. before 29 March 1515 (Salis., Reg. Audley f. 66b; *Cal. MSS. D. & C. Wells* II 239).

M. Thomas Lovel D.Cn.L. 1515.
Occ. 6 July 1515 (*Reg. King* p. 175).

M. James Fitzjames D.Th. 1524–1541.
Coll. 14 Nov. 1524 (*Reg. Bps., 1518–1559* p. 37). D. before 22 March 1541 (*ibid.* p. 91).

Edward Rogers 1541–?
Coll. 4 July 1541 (*Reg. Bps., 1518–1559* p. 91).

PREBENDARIES OF YATTON

M. Anthony de Lavenza 1306.
M. Richard de Abyndon ?–1322.
Lavenza occ. 18 Jan. 1306, claimed preb. in Wells by virtue of prov. (*CPL.* II 18). Probably preb. of Yatton since Abyndon then said to be unlawfully detaining preb. (*ibid.* pp. 18–19) and Abyndon occ. as preb. of Yatton 6 Dec. 1308 (*Reg. of W. Reynolds*, ed. R. A. Wilson (Worcs. Hist. Soc., 1927) p. 161). D. as preb. before 20 March 1322 (Reg. Drokensford f. 180).

Andrew de Drokensford 1322–1326.

Richard de Thistleden ?–1325.

M. Robert de Baldock *senior* D.C.L. 1324–1327.

Richard de Drokensford 1326–1328.

M. Thomas de Trillek M.A. 1327–1364.

M. Alan de Cosneburg D.C.L. 1327–1330.

M. Robert de Stratford M.A. 1328–1334.

Andrew de Drokensford coll. 20 March 1322 (Reg. Drokensford f. 180). Royal gr. to Baldock 19 Sept. 1324 (*CPR. 1324–1327* p. 24). Royal prohibn. 3 May 1325 against all ecclesiastical persons taking proceedings against judgt. where k. recovered right to pres. to preb. (*ibid.* pp. 116–17). Res. of Thistleden from preb. ordered 9 May, mand. to install Baldock 15 May (*Reg. Drokensford* p. 245). Baldock does not appear to have obtained possession since Andrew de Drokensford res. preb. before 19 Oct. 1326 when Richard de Drokensford coll. by bp. (*ibid.* p. 252). Baldock cited by bp. 14 Nov. because still claiming preb. (*ibid.*). Baldock d. 28 May 1327 (Murimuth, *Chronica*, ed. T. Hog (Eng. Hist. Soc., 1846) p. 51). Trillek prov. 14 July (*CPL.* II 263), but prov. to Cosneburg 22 Nov., 23 Jan. 1328 and 2 May (*ibid.* pp. 267, 272). Prov. to Cosneburg probably made because Trillek then said to be under age and not in priest's orders (*CPP.* I 114–15). Richard de Drokensford appears to have held preb. in spite of prov. to Trillek and Cosneburg since res. before 25 July when Stratford coll. by bp. (*Reg. Drokensford* p. 290). Litigation at curia between Trillek, Stratford and Cosneburg about preb., but Cosneburg renounced claims c. 25 Feb. 1330 when prov. to canonry in York (*CPL.* II 306). Stratford probably res. claims to preb. 1334 when prov. to deanery of Wells (*ibid.* p. 402). Trillek remained in possession, estate ratif. 28 Aug. 1347 (*CPR. 1345–1348* p. 552). Bp. of Rochester 1364.

John de Sleford 1370–1401.

Royal gr. 8 Sept. 1370 (*CPR. 1367–1370* p. 462). Estate ratif. 17 Nov. 1372 (*CPR. 1370–1374* p. 212). D. before 22 Nov. 1401 (*Reg. Giffard and Bowet* p. 23).

Thomas Langley 1401–1406.

Coll. 22 Nov. 1401 (*Reg. Giffard and Bowet* p. 23). Bp. of Durham 1406.

M. John Prophete 1406.

Exch. preb. with John Mackworth for preb. of Combe Quinta, 23 Aug. 1406 (*Reg. Giffard and Bowet* p. 60).

John Mackworth 1406–1451.

By exch. Aug. 1406. Royal gr. 22 Sept. (*CPR. 1405–1408* p. 224). Adm. 22 Oct. (*Reg. Giffard and Bowet* p. 65). D. before 29 Sept. 1451 (*Reg. Bekynton* I 171).

M. Thomas Purveour M.A. 1451–?

Coll. 29 Sept. 1451 (*Reg. Bekynton* I 171). Occ. 14 June 1466 (*Reg. Stillington* pp. 4–5). ? Held preb. until d. before 5 Oct. 1469 (*CPL.* XII 350–1).[1]

M. Richard Nix D.Cn. & C.L. ?–1494.

Occ. 21 May 1488 (*Reg. Stillington* p. 151). Archdcn. of Wells 1494.

M. Robert Middelton D.C.L. 1494–1499.

Coll. 16 July 1494 (*Reg. Stillington* pp. 192–3). Adm. 24 July (*Cal. MSS. D. & C. Wells* II 136). D. before 28 Nov. 1499 (*ibid.* p. 156).

M. Jerome Boerio D.Cn. & C.L. 1499–1506.

Adm. 28 Nov. 1499 (*Cal. MSS. D. & C. Wells* II 156). D. before 31 July 1506 (*ibid.* p. 195).

[1] This preb. was possibly held by Walter Buk on the d. of Purveour. See p. 65, n. 1.

M. Bernard Boerio 1506–?
Adm. 31 July 1506 (*Cal. MSS. D. & C. Wells* II 195). Occ. 1509 (*Reg. King* p. 138).

M. John Taylour D.Cn.L. 1522.
Occ. 14 Jan. 1522 (*Reg. Bps., 1518–1559* p. 19). ? Held preb. until d. 1 Oct./24 Nov. 1534 (PCC 20 Hogen).

Thomas Leson 1535.
Occ. 1535 (*Valor* I 135).

UNIDENTIFIED PREBENDARIES

John de Mettingham ?–1301.
Vac. preb. in Wells before 22 June 1301 (Reg. I f. 122).

John de Godeley 1301–?
Coll. to preb. vac. by Mettingham 22 June 1301 (Reg. I f. 122). Adm. by proxy 24 Sept. (*Cal. MSS. D. & C. Wells* I 159).

Thomas de Charlton ?–1302.
Res. preb. in Wells before 28 June 1302 (*CPR. 1301–1307* p. 41).

Stephen de Brawode 1302–?
Royal gr. 28 June 1302 of preb. vac. by Charlton (*CPR. 1301–1307* p. 41).

John de Cadomo ?–1310.
Vac. preb. in Wells 9 Apr. 1310 (Reg. Drokensford f. 30b).

Peter de Brigencourt 1310–?
Coll. to preb. held by Cadomo 9 Apr. 1310 (Reg. Drokensford f. 30b).

M. Nicholas de Welles ?–1311.
Res. preb. in Wells before 20 June 1311 (Reg. Drokensford f. 36b).

Nicholas Waryn 1311–1319.
Coll. 20 June 1311 to preb. held by Welles (Reg. Drokensford f. 36b). Res. before 13 Aug. 1319 (*ibid.* f. 123). (See below, Michael de Eston, p. 82.)

M. Henry de Bray ?–1312.
D. as preb. of Wells before 18 Apr. 1312 (Reg. Drokensford f. 40).

M. I. de Roos 1312–?
Coll. 18 Apr. 1312 to preb. held by Bray (Reg. Drokensford f. 40).

Adam Osgodby ?–1316.
D. as preb. of Wells before 1 Sept. 1316 (Reg. Drokensford f. 40).

John Maitel 1316–?
Coll. to preb. held by Osgodby 1 Sept. 1316 (Reg. Drokensford f. 40).

M. James de Cobeham D.Cn.L. ?–1318.
Vac. preb. in Wells before 18 Jan. 1318 (Reg. Drokensford f. 152).

M. Richard de Stanhowe 1318–?
Coll. 18 Jan. 1318 to preb. held by Cobeham (Reg. Drokensford f. 152).

William de Lanton ?–1319.
D. as preb. of Wells before 13 Aug. 1319 (Reg. Drokensford f. 123b).

M. Richard de Forde D.C.L. 1319–?
Coll. 13 Aug. 1319 to preb. held by Lanton (Reg. Drokensford f. 123b).

G

Michael de Eston 1319-?
Coll. to preb. held by Nicholas Waryn, 13 Aug. 1319 (Reg. Drokensford f. 123).
(See above, p. 81.)

Walter de Bedewynde ?-1321.
Res. preb. in Wells before 8 Jan. 1321 (Reg. Drokensford f. 160).

Michael Beneyt 1321-?
Coll. 8 Jan. 1321 to preb. held by Bedewynde (Reg. Drokensford f. 160).

John de Briguencourt 1323.
Occ. as preb. of Wells 3 Dec. 1323 (*CPL*. II 236).

William de Burne ?-1323.
D. as preb. of Wells before 23 Dec. 1323 (Reg. Drokensford f. 201b).

Thomas de Stapleton 1323-?
Coll. 23 Dec. 1323 to preb. held by Burne (Reg. Drokensford f. 201b).

M. **Richard Abel** M.A. ?-1327.
D. as can. and preb. of Wells Oct. 1327 (*Cal. MSS. D. & C. Wells* II 4).

Philip de Daventre 1330.
Prov. to canonry and preb. in Wells 16 Sept. 1330 (*CPL*. II 312).

Nicholas de Maunham 1343.
Petition gr. 18 Oct. 1343 for canonry and preb. of Wells (*CPP*. I 22).

M. **Robert Middelond** D.Th. 1362.
Prov. to canonry of Wells with reservn. of preb. 7 March 1349 (*CPL*. III 295). Said
to hold monetary preb. of eight marks in Wells 21 Nov. 1362 (*CPP*. I 386).

Nicholas de Coleshull 1349.
Occ. as bursal preb. of Wells 29 May 1349 (*CPL*. II 295).

Thomas Madefrey 1363.
Occ. as preb. of Wells 31 Aug. 1363 (*CPP*. I 455).

M. **Thomas Frome** B.C.L. 1386.
Occ. as can. and preb. of Wells 1386 (*Cal. MSS. D. & C. Wells* I 297, 605; II 784).

John de Maydenhith 1400.
Occ. as can. and preb. of Wells 25 June 1400 (Worcester, Reg. Tideman f. 43b).

M. **John de Tyssebury** B.C.L. 1402.
Occ. as can. and preb. of Wells 1402 (*Cal. MSS. D. & C. Wells* II 654).

PREBENDARIES OF COMBE

John Wakering 1404.
Occ. as preb. of Combe 13 Nov. 1404 (*CPL*. VI 57).

Walter Shiryngton 1409.
Occ. as preb. of Combe 1409 (*CPL*. VI 210).

Richard Penyfader 1423.
Occ. as preb. of Combe 1 Aug. 1423 (*Reg. Bubwith* II 430).

PREBENDARIES OF WEDMORE

Robert Strotton ?-1397/8.
D. as preb. of Wedmore Sept. 1397/8 (*Cal. MSS. D. & C. Wells* II 31).

M. Henry Sharp D.C.L. ?–1472.
Res. preb. of Wedmore[1] 1472 when preb. of Dultingcote (*Reg. Stillington* pp. 94–5).

M. William Chokke 1472–?
Coll. to preb. of Wedmore held by Sharp, 20 Oct. 1472 (*Reg. Stillington* pp. 94–5).

PERSONS PROVIDED TO A CANONRY IN WELLS WITH EXPECTATION OF A PREBEND

Hugh Ricardi 1316.
Prov. 17 Nov. 1316 (*CPL.* II 133).

M. Ralph de Salopia D.Th., D.Cn.L. 1317–1329.
Prov. 21 July 1317 (*CPL.* II 165). Can. of Wells 1329 when el. bp. of Bath and Wells (*Chartularies of Bath* II 72; *Reg. R. de Salopia* I p. xvii).

M. Elias de Walwayn M.A. 1330, 1331.
Prov. 7 June 1330 (*CPL.* II 317). Adm. to canonry 8 Feb. 1331 (*Reg. R. de Salopia* I 85).

Ralph de Bondeby 1348.
Occ. 21 June 1348 (*CPP.* I 132).

M. John Thursteyn B.C.L. 1348.
Prov. 20 Nov. 1348 (*CPL.* III 294).

John de Horsington 1349.
Prov. 29 Apr. 1349 (*CPL.* III 295).

---

[1] Sharp possibly held the preb. of Wedmore Quinta. He is stated (*Emden, Reg. Ox.* III 1679) to have held the preb. of Wedmore Prima, but this was attached to the deanery.

G *

APPENDIX

Note on the order of the dignitaries

The order of the dignitaries in this volume has presented some problems, since there were two alternative orders in which the dignitaries sat, their order in chapter and in choir.

1. *Order in chapter.*	2. *Order in choir.*
Dean	Dean
Precentor	Precentor
Archdcn. of Wells	Archdcn. of Wells
Treasurer	Archdcn. of Bath
Chancellor	Chancellor
Archdcn. of Bath	Treasurer
Archdcn. of Taunton	Archdcn. of Taunton
Abbot of Muchelney	Abbot of Muchelney
Abbot of Bec	Abbot of Athelney
Abbot of Athelney	(*Wells Cathedral: its foundation,*
Subdean	*constitutional history and statutes,*
Succentor	ed. H. E. Reynolds (Leeds, 1880)
Provost	pp. 1–2).

(K. Edwards, *English Secular Cathedrals* (Manchester, 1949) p. 178n).

For the convenience of the reader the dignitaries have been arranged with the archdeacons together and the abbots listed in accordance with their prebends, and a similar rule has been observed for the provost since he held the prebend of Combe Duodecima.

There was similar difficulty in deciding on an arrangement for the fifty-five cathedral prebends, but since so many of the prebends have the same name, e.g. fifteen Combes, five Wedmores and two Milvertons and since several alternative and seemingly arbitrary arrangements of the prebends have been found in different authorities, it was decided, with the permission of the late Dean Woodforde, that the prebends should be listed in alphabetical order. The Diocesan Handbook has been used as a guide to the names of the prebends, with the exception of those which no longer exist, e.g. Long Sutton, North Curry, etc. in which cases the modern place name has been used. Two different orders in which the prebends are found are listed below; the first is the list given in Hardy's edition of Le Neve's *Fasti*, the second is the one made in 1298, on the authority of Dean Haselschawe, to show the distribution of the daily Psalms among the different prebendaries.

Dean Haselschawe's list is printed in 'Prebendal Stalls and Misericords in the Cathedral church of Wells', by C. M. Church (*Archaeologia* iv 319–42). It is noted in this article that the names of the Wells prebends were listed in another order when they were assessed for taxation in 1291 by commissioners of Pope Nicholas IV. Yet another order can be found in the *Valor Ecclesiasticus*.

1. *Le Neve-Hardy's List.*   **2. *Dean Haselschawe's List.***

Warminster alias Luxfield	Wedmore I
Ilton	Cleeve
Barton David	St Decumans
Timberscomb	Combe I
Worminster	Combe XII
Eastharptree	Compton (Bishop)
Wedmore (2nd)	Yatton
Wedmore (3rd)	Haselbere
Wedmore (4th)	Wandstrow
Wedmore (5th)	Scalford
Haselbere	Wedmore II
Buckland and Dynham	Combe II
Whitelackington	Combe III
Ashill	Combe IV
Henstridge	Buckland (Dinham)
Easton in Gordano	Milverton I
Cudworth	Henstridge
Milverton (2nd)	Timberscombe
Dyndre	Ashill
Holcombe	Combe V
Taunton	Easton (in Gordano)
Wanstraw	Ilton
S. Decuman	Combe XIII
Lytton	(Compton) Dundon
Cumpton Dundon	Combe XIV
Yatton	Combe VI
Shalford alias Scamford	Dultingcote
Wiveliscombe	Taunton
Compton Bishop	(Huish and) Brent
Dultincote alias Fingherst	Wiveliscombe
Combe (1st)	Ilminster
Combe (2nd)	Long Sutton
Combe (3rd)	Wormenster alias Luxville
Combe (4th)	Combe VII
Combe (5th)	North Curry
Combe (6th)	Wormenster
Combe (7th)	Whitelackington
Combe (8th)	Combe XV
Combe (9th)	Milverton II
Combe (10th)	Wedmore II
Combe (11th)	Barton
Combe (12th)	Combe VIII
Combe (13th)	Wedmore IV
Combe (14th)	Cudworth
Combe (15th)	Combe IX
	Combe X
	Whitchurch
	Eastharptree
	Combe XI
	Wedmore V
	Dinder

Index

PERSONS

PLACES